Legacy Library

The Psychology of Marketing

Author: Suhail Akhtar

Published independently by the author.
Suhail Akhtar

DISCLAIMER

This ebook is provided for educational and informational purposes only.The author is not a financial advisor, legal advisor, or business consultant.Any strategies, tips, or examples mentioned in this ebook are based on personal research and experience.Results may vary from person to person. The author does not guarantee any specific income, profit, or success.Readers are advised to do their own research and take responsibility for their actions before applying any information from this ebook.By reading this ebook, you agree that the author is not responsible for any losses, damages, or legal issues that may occur

TABLE OF CONTENTS

1

Introduction

Marketing ek aisa concept hai jo har business ki backbone hota hai, lekin aksar log ise sirf “selling” ya “advertising” samajh lete hain. Reality me marketing ka matlab sirf product bechna nahi, balki customer ko samajhna aur uski zarurat ke according solution dena hota hai.

Simple shabdon me samjhe to marketing ka matlab hai — **sahi product ko sahi insaan tak, sahi waqt par, sahi tarike se pahunchana**.

Maan lijiye ek insaan ko bhook lagi hai. Us samay agar uske saamne uski pasand ka khana aa jaye, to wo bina soche kharid lega. Ye jo understanding hai — ki customer kya chahta hai aur kab chahta hai — isi ko marketing kehte hain.

Why Good Products Fail Without Marketing

Bahut baar aisa hota hai ki product quality me best hota hai, phir bhi wo market me nahi bikta. Iska reason simple hai — **logon ko uske baare me pata hi nahi hota, ya wo usse connect nahi kar paate**.

Sochiye aapne ek bahut acchi ebook banayi, lekin aapne uska promotion nahi kiya. Na kisi ko bataya, na social media par share kiya. Result? Chahe product kitna bhi accha ho, sale nahi hogi.
Dusri taraf, ek average product agar smart marketing ke saath present kiya jaye — attractive design, clear messaging aur strong branding ke saath — to wo zyada bik sakta hai.
Isliye kaha jata hai:
"A great product without marketing is like a shop in the desert."

Marketing vs Advertising
Marketing aur advertising ko aksar ek hi samjha jata hai, lekin in dono me basic difference hota hai.
Marketing ek complete process hai jisme customer ko samajhna, product design karna, uski pricing decide karna, aur use market me launch karna shamil hota hai.
Wahin advertising, marketing ka sirf ek hissa hai jiska kaam hota hai product ke baare me logon tak information pahunchana aur unka attention attract karna.
Example ke liye, agar aap ek juice brand launch karte hain, to uska flavor decide karna, bottle design banana aur price set karna — ye sab marketing hai. Lekin us juice ka

Instagram ya YouTube par ad chalana — ye advertising hai.

Final Insight

Aaj ke competitive world me sirf accha product banana kaafi nahi hai. Success ke liye zaruri hai ki aap apne customer ko samjhein, uski problem solve karein, aur apni value ko clearly communicate karein.

Yahi marketing ka essence hai —

“Not just selling a product, but creating a desire to buy.”

2

Why Most Products Fail

Agar tum dhyaan se dekho, duniya mein hazaaron products har saal launch hote hain… lekin unmein se bahut saare quietly disappear ho jaate hain.

Na unka naam yaad rehta hai, na unka koi impact.

Sawal yeh hai — **aisa kyun hota hai?**

Kya wo products bure hote hain?

Zaroori nahi.

Asal problem aksar product mein nahi, balki uske peeche ki **soch aur samajh** mein hoti hai.

Chalo ise ek simple kahani se samajhte hain…

Maan lo ek chhota bachcha hai, jo apni taraf se ek bahut hi sundar drawing banata hai.

Usse lagta hai ki ye duniya ki sabse best drawing hai.

Lekin jab wo usse dusron ko dikhata hai, koi usme interest nahi leta।

Ab kya drawing galat thi?

Nahi.

Bas usne yeh nahi samjha ki dusre log kya dekhna chahte hain।

Bilkul isi tarah, businesses bhi yahi galti karte hain।

❖ Research ki kami – Andhere mein faisla

Bahut saare log excitement mein product bana dete hain, lekin ye check hi nahi karte ki market mein uski demand hai ya nahi।

Wo assume kar lete hain ki:

"Jo mujhe acha lagta hai, wo sabko acha lagega."

Lekin reality alag hoti hai।

Socho tumne ek bahut hi achha raincoat design kiya।

Material strong hai, design stylish hai, sab perfect hai।

Ab tum usse bechne jaate ho ek aise area mein jahan barish bahut kam hoti hai।

Kya hoga?

Log kahenge — "Humein iski zarurat hi nahi hai।"

Yahan product galat nahi tha,

decision galat tha।

Research ka simple matlab hota hai:

pehle samajhna… phir banana।

❖ Customer ki need na samajhna – Galat problem solve karna

Business ka sabse important rule hai:

Product nahi, problem becho.

Log product nahi kharidte,

wo apni problem ka solution kharidte hain।

Maan lo ek aadmi ko tez bhook lagi hai I
Agar tum usko ek expensive headphone offer kar do,
toh kya wo kharidega?
Nahi I
Us moment par uski need sirf khana hai I
Isi tarah, bahut saare creators aur sellers apni pasand ke hisaab se product bana dete hain I
Wo sochte hain — "Ye feature add kar dete hain, ye design bana dete hain…"
Lekin wo ye nahi sochte ki:
Customer actually chahta kya hai?
Result?
Product use hi nahi hota I
Aur dheere-dheere market se gayab ho jaata hai I

❖ Galat audience ya galat jagah – Sahi cheez, galat log

Kabhi-kabhi product bilkul perfect hota hai,
lekin usse galat logon ko becha jaata hai I
Maan lo tum ek premium smartphone bech rahe ho,
jiski price bahut zyada hai I
Agar tum usse aise area mein promote karoge jahan log basic zarooraton ke liye struggle kar rahe hain,
toh kya wo kharidenge?
Shayad nahi I
Kyuki unki priority kuch aur hai I

Isi tarah, agar tum bachchon ke toys ko corporate office mein bechne jao,

toh koi interest nahi lega ।

Yahan problem product nahi hai,

target galat hai ।

Business mein ek simple rule hota hai:

Har product ka ek "perfect customer" hota hai.

Agar tum usse nahi dhoondh paaye, toh product fail ho jayega ।

Jab hum thoda aur deeply dekhte hain,

toh pata chalta hai ki har successful product ke peeche ek strong connection hota hai —

Product + Market + Customer = Perfect Match

Isse hi simple language mein kehte hain:

"Product-Market Fit"

Agar tumhara product market ki demand ke saath match nahi karta,

toh chahe tum kitni bhi marketing kar lo…

long-term success milna mushkil hai ।

Isi ke saath ek aur important concept aata hai —

Customer Persona

Matlab tumhe clearly pata hona chahiye:

tumhara customer kaun hai,

wo kya sochta hai,

wo kis problem se pareshan hai,

aur wo kis solution ke liye paise dene ko ready hai ।

Jab tak ye clarity nahi aati,
tab tak product banana sirf guessing game hi rahega।
Zyada tar products isliye fail nahi hote kyunki wo bure hote hain…
balki isliye fail hote hain kyunki unhe samajh ke bina banaya jaata hai। Isliye hamesha yaad rakho:

"Product banana aasaan hai,
lekin sahi product banana ek samajh ka khel hai।"

Aur jab tum samajh jaate ho —
market ko, customer ko, aur unki problem ko…
Tab success sirf ek possibility nahi,
ek natural result ban jaata hai। 🚀

3

Understanding Customer Psychology

Jab bhi hum marketing ki duniya me enter karte hain, to sabse pehla aur sabse powerful concept hota hai customer psychology, yani grahak ke dimaag aur uski soch ko samajhna. Bahut log yahan galti karte hain ki wo sirf product par focus karte hain—kaisa product hai, kitna strong hai, kya features hain—lekin asli game product ka nahi, balki customer ke mind ka hota hai. Sach to ye hai ki duniya ka sabse average product bhi bik sakta hai agar aap customer psychology samajh jaate hain, aur duniya ka best product bhi fail ho sakta hai agar aapko ye nahi pata ki log sochte kaise hain aur kharidte kaise hain. Marketing ka matlab sirf bechna nahi hota, balki kisi insaan ke mind me ek aisi desire create karna hota hai jisse wo khud aapka product lena chahe.

Sabse pehle samajhte hain ki log kharidte kyun hain, kyunki ye pura chapter isi foundation par based hai. Log kabhi bhi product ke liye paisa nahi dete, wo apni problem ke solution ke liye paisa dete hain, ya phir ek better feeling ke liye. Har insaan ke andar kuch desires hoti hain—jaise comfort, status, safety, happiness, attraction, ya respect—and jab koi product inme se kisi ek desire ko fulfill karta hai, tab purchase hota hai. Example ke liye, jab koi insaan ek costly branded watch kharidta hai, to wo sirf time dekhne ke liye nahi kharid raha hota, balki wo apne status aur personality ko show karne ke liye kharid raha hota hai, ya jab koi insaan gym membership leta hai, to wo sirf exercise ke liye nahi, balki apne body ko better banane aur confidence gain karne ke liye invest karta hai. Isi tarah jab koi insaan online course kharidta hai, to wo sirf knowledge nahi le raha hota, balki apni future life ko improve karne ki hope kharid raha hota hai.

Iska matlab ye hua ki har purchase ke peeche ek visible reason hota hai aur ek hidden emotional reason hota hai, aur successful marketer wahi hota hai jo is hidden reason ko samajh le. Customer kabhi seedha nahi bolta ki wo kis emotion ke liye kharid raha hai, lekin uske actions sab kuch bata dete hain. Jaise koi insaan ek normal phone ke bajaye ek premium smartphone choose karta hai kyunki usse lagta hai ki ye uski personality ko match karta hai aur usse ek alag identity deta hai, ya jab koi insaan apne ghar ke liye expensive furniture leta hai, to wo sirf comfort nahi balki ek premium lifestyle feel karna chahta hai. Yani product sirf ek medium hota hai, asli cheez hoti hai feeling.

Ab baat karte hain emotion vs logic ki, jo customer psychology ka sabse important aur powerful part hai. Log aksar bolte hain ki wo logical decisions lete hain, lekin reality me 90% decisions emotional hote hain aur baaki 10% me logic ka use hota hai sirf us decision ko justify karne ke liye. Yani pehle dil decision leta hai aur baad me dimaag usse support karta hai. Example ke liye, jab koi insaan ek iPhone kharidta hai, to wo pehle uske brand, design aur premium feel se attract hota hai (emotion), aur baad me wo justify karta hai ki isme security achhi hai, camera strong hai aur performance best hai (logic). Isi tarah jab koi insaan ek particular dress kharidta hai, to wo pehle usse pasand aati hai aur usse imagine karta hai ki wo isme kaisa dikhega (emotion), aur phir wo bolta hai ki ye comfortable hai aur quality achhi hai (logic).

Emotion decision ko trigger karta hai, aur logic us decision ko safe feel karata hai. Agar aap sirf logical marketing karte hain—jaise features, specifications, data— to aap customer ko impress to kar sakte hain lekin convince nahi kar sakte. Lekin agar aap emotion ko target karte hain—jaise feeling, desire, fear, excitement— to aap customer ko action lene par majboor kar dete hain. Jaise agar aap bolte hain “ye product 20% faster hai,” to ye logic hai, lekin agar aap bolte hain “ye product aapka kaam aadha time me khatam kar dega aur aapko extra free time dega,” to ye emotion hai, aur yahi difference sale create karta hai. Isi liye bade brands apni ads me numbers se zyada stories aur emotions use karte hain.

Emotion ke andar bhi kai powerful triggers hote hain jaise fear, greed, happiness, belongingness, aur pride. Fear ka matlab hota hai kisi cheez ko lose karne ka darr, jaise insurance companies isi emotion ka use karti hain jab wo dikhati hain ki agar aapne insurance nahi liya to future me problem ho sakti hai, greed ka matlab hota hai zyada paane ki ichha, jaise "limited time offer" ya "extra discount" dekh kar log turant attract hote hain, happiness ka matlab hota hai achha feel karna, jaise chocolates ya gifts log khushi ke liye kharidte hain, belongingness ka matlab hota hai kisi group ka part banna, jaise branded clothes pehen kar log ek certain class me belong karna chahte hain, aur pride ka matlab hota hai apne aap par garv feel karna, jaise koi insaan apni achievement celebrate karne ke liye luxury item kharidta hai.

Ab aate hain curiosity effect par, jo ek silent but extremely powerful weapon hai marketing me. Insaan ki natural tendency hoti hai ki wo unknown cheezon ko jaan na chahta hai, aur jab usse lagta hai ki usse kuch important ya interesting miss ho raha hai, to wo automatically uski taraf attract hota hai. Isi ko curiosity kehte hain, aur smart marketers isko bahut intelligently use karte hain. Jab aap kisi cheez ko poora reveal nahi karte aur thoda suspense create karte hain, to log uske baare me aur jaan na chahte hain. Jaise agar aap likhte hain "Ye 1 simple habit aapki life completely change kar sakti hai," to insaan turant sochta hai ki wo habit kya hai, ya jab koi YouTube video ka title hota hai "I tried this for 7 days and the result shocked me," to log curiosity ke chakkar me click karte hain.

Curiosity effect ka ek aur strong form hota hai incomplete information, jahan aap intentionally sab kuch nahi batate, jisse customer ka mind khud baaki gap fill karne ki koshish karta hai. Jaise agar koi product page par likha ho "Only 3 items left," to insaan sochta hai ki shayad ye product demand me hai aur agar abhi nahi liya to chance miss ho jayega, ya jab koi course kehta hai "Limited seats available," to log jaldi decision lete hain. Isi tarah jab aap kisi story ko aadha chhod dete hain, to reader naturally uska end jaan na chahta hai, aur yahi principle marketing me use hota hai.

Curiosity ka use sirf attention grab karne ke liye nahi hota, balki engagement aur conversion badhane ke liye bhi hota hai. Jab aap customer ko ek journey par le jaate hain jahan wo step by step cheezon ko discover karta hai, to uska interest bana rehta hai aur wo aapke saath connected feel karta hai. Jaise email marketing me pehle ek hook diya jata hai, phir next mail me thodi aur information, aur finally product offer diya jata hai, jisse customer gradually convince hota hai.

Agar aap in teeno concepts—log kyun kharidte hain, emotion vs logic, aur curiosity effect—ko deeply samajh lete hain, to aap marketing ke core ko samajh jaate hain. Phir aap sirf product bechne ki koshish nahi karte, balki aap customer ke mind me ek aisi positioning create karte hain jahan aapka product unke liye ek natural choice ban jata hai. Aapko push nahi karna padta, aapko convince nahi karna padta, balki customer khud aapke paas aata hai kyunki usse lagta hai ki ye product uske liye bana hai.

Is chapter ka final conclusion ye hai ki marketing ka asli game product banana nahi, balki customer ko samajhna hai. Jitna aap customer ke emotions, desires, fears aur curiosity ko samajhoge, utna hi aap powerful marketer banoge. Aur jab aap ye samajh jaate hain ki insaan ka decision process kaise kaam karta hai, tab selling ek struggle nahi rehti, balki ek natural flow ban jata hai jahan har cheez smoothly convert hoti hai. Yahi customer psychology ka magic hai, aur yahi successful marketing ki real foundation hai.

4

Finding the Right Target Audience

Marketing ki duniya me sabse badi galti jo beginners karte hain wo ye hoti hai ki wo apna product “sabke liye” bana dete hain, aur sach ye hai ki jo product sabke liye hota hai wo aksar kisi ke liye bhi special nahi hota, isi wajah se wo market me fail ho jata hai. Is chapter ka core concept ye hai ki agar aapko apna product sell karna hai, to sabse pehle aapko ye samajhna padega ki aapka *real customer kaun hai*, kyunki jab tak aapko ye nahi pata hoga ki aap kis problem ko solve kar rahe hain aur kis type ke logon ke liye kar rahe hain, tab tak aapka marketing message weak rahega aur aapka product ignore ho jayega.

Sabse pehle samajhte hain ki **Target Audience kya hoti hai**. Simple language me, target audience wo specific group of people hote hain jo aapke product ya service ko kharidne ke sabse jyada chances rakhte hain, matlab wo log jinko aapka product dekhkar lagta hai ki “haan ye mere kaam ka hai”, jaise agar aap ek online course bana rahe hain jo Amazon selling sikhata hai to aapka target audience wo log honge jo online earning karna chahte hain, side income banana chahte hain ya apna business start karna chahte hain, na ki wo log jo already ek successful offline business chala rahe hain aur online me interested hi nahi hain.

Yahan ek important baat samajhni hai ki target audience ko define karna sirf age ya gender tak limited nahi hota, balki usme unki problems, desires, lifestyle aur behavior bhi include hota hai, jaise agar aap gym products sell kar rahe hain to aapka target audience sirf “18–30 saal ke ladke” nahi hai, balki wo log hain jo apni body improve karna chahte hain, fit rehna chahte hain aur apne confidence ko boost karna chahte hain, matlab aapko unke mindset ko samajhna hai.

Ab sawal aata hai ki **sahi customer kaise pehchanein**, kyunki ye sabse crucial step hai. Iske liye sabse pehle aapko ek simple sa rule follow karna hai: “Problem → Solution → People”, matlab pehle aap ek specific problem identify karo, fir uska solution banao, aur fir dekho ki wo problem kin logon ko hoti hai, wahi aapka target audience hai, jaise agar problem hai “logon ko weight loss me dikkat ho rahi hai” aur aapka solution hai “home workout program”, to aapka target audience wo log honge jo busy hain, gym nahi ja pa rahe hain aur ghar par hi fit hona chahte hain.

Ek aur powerful tarika hai target audience identify karne ka, jise kehte hain **Customer Avatar banana**, matlab aap apne ideal customer ka ek imaginary profile create karte hain, jisme aap uska naam, age, job, income, problems, goals sab define karte hain, jaise aap imagine kar sakte hain “Rahul, 25 saal ka hai, job karta hai, salary 25,000 hai, wo side income banana chahta hai lekin usko pata nahi kaha se start kare”, ab jab aap aise specific customer ko mind me rakhkar content ya product banate hain, to aapka message direct uske dil tak pahuchta hai.

Ab baat karte hain ek bahut powerful concept ki jo aaj ke time me marketing ka game change kar raha hai, aur wo hai **Niche Marketing**. Niche ka matlab hota hai ek specific, chhota aur focused segment of market, matlab aap “bade market” me compete karne ke bajay “chhote aur specific group” ko target karte ho, jaise agar aap “fitness” market me enter karte ho to competition bahut jyada hai, lekin agar aap “weight loss for working women after pregnancy” jaise niche ko target karte ho to aap ek specific problem solve kar rahe ho aur aap easily apni identity bana sakte ho.

Niche marketing ka sabse bada benefit ye hota hai ki aapka competition kam ho jata hai aur aap apne audience ke liye expert ban jate ho, jabki broad market me aap sirf ek aur option ban kar reh jate ho, jaise ek general clothing brand banana mushkil hai lekin "budget-friendly formal shirts for college students" jaisa niche target karna asaan hai kyunki aap exactly jante ho ki aap kiske liye bana rahe ho.

Ek aur important cheez jo aapko samajhni hai wo ye hai ki **jab aap sabko target karte ho to aap kisi ko bhi effectively target nahi kar pate**, kyunki har customer ka need alag hota hai aur ek hi message sab par kaam nahi karta, jaise agar aap ek hi ad me students, housewives aur businessmen sabko target karne ki koshish karoge to aapka message confusing ho jayega aur koi bhi strongly connect nahi karega.

Ab real world me dekhein to bade bade brands bhi isi principle ko follow karte hain, jaise ek smartphone company alag-alag segment ke liye alag products banati hai jaise budget users ke liye affordable phone aur gamers ke liye high-performance phone, ek hi product sabko satisfy nahi karta, isi liye segmentation aur targeting bahut important hota hai.

Target audience ko samajhne ke liye aapko unke behavior ko observe karna bhi zaroori hai, jaise wo kaha time spend karte hain, kya dekhte hain, kya search karte hain, kaunsi problems unhe disturb karti hain, kyunki jab aapko ye sab clear hota hai to aap apna marketing message unke according design kar pate hain aur unhe feel hota hai ki "ye product mere liye hi bana hai".

Ek aur powerful strategy hai **feedback aur testing**, matlab aap apne product ya idea ko chhote level par test karo aur dekho kaun log interest dikha rahe hain, unse feedback lo aur uske basis par apne target audience ko refine karo, kyunki practical data hamesha assumptions se better hota hai.

Yahan ek mistake jo aapko avoid karni hai wo ye hai ki aap sirf "demographics" par focus na karein, jaise age, gender, location, balki "psychographics" par bhi dhyan dein, matlab unki thinking, beliefs, desires aur fears ko samjhein, kyunki log logical reasons se kam aur emotional reasons se jyada purchase karte hain, jaise koi insaan gym membership isliye nahi leta ki usse muscles banane hain, balki isliye leta hai kyunki wo confident feel karna chahta hai aur attractive dikhna chahta hai.

Agar aap apni ebook, product ya business ko successful banana chahte hain, to aapko ek simple formula yaad rakhna hoga: **"Right Product + Right Audience + Right Message = Successful Marketing"**, aur isme sabse pehla aur important step hai "Right Audience", kyunki agar audience hi galat hai to best product bhi fail ho jayega.

Aakhir me, ek line jo aapko hamesha yaad rakhni chahiye wo ye hai ki marketing ka game "zyada logon tak pahuchne ka nahi, balki sahi logon tak pahuchne ka hai", jab aap apne ideal customer ko clearly samajh lete hain aur unke problems ko deeply solve karte hain, tab aapko apna product push karne ki zarurat nahi padti, balki customers khud aapke paas aate hain.

Yahi hai **Finding the Right Target Audience** ka asli power, aur agar aapne is concept ko deeply samajh liya, to aap apne kisi bhi product ko sahi direction me le ja sakte hain aur market me strong position bana sakte hain.

5

Creating Demand Before Selling

Marketing ki duniya ka ek golden rule hai — "Sell karne se pehle demand create karo", lekin beginners yahan sabse badi galti kar dete hain, wo direct product lekar market me aa jate hain aur expect karte hain ki log turant kharid lenge, jabki reality ye hai ki log kisi unknown cheez ko bina interest ke kabhi nahi kharidte, isliye agar aapko long term me success chahiye to aapko selling se pehle logon ke dimaag me "chahat" paida karni padegi, matlab aisa environment banana padega jahan customer khud aapke product ke liye excited ho jaye aur bole "mujhe ye chahiye".

Sabse pehle basic samajhte hain ki demand hoti kya hai, simple shabdon me demand ka matlab hota hai kisi cheez ko paane ki strong desire, jab kisi insaan ko lagta hai ki koi product uski life ko better bana sakta hai ya uski problem solve kar sakta hai, tab wo us product ko lene ke liye ready hota hai, lekin agar usko ye feeling hi nahi aayi to chahe

aap kitni bhi advertisement chala lo wo ignore hi karega, isi liye smart marketers pehle logon ke mind me problem highlight karte hain aur phir uska solution apne product ke through dikhate hain.
Ab yahan ek bahut powerful concept aata hai — "Artificial Demand", iska matlab hota hai aisi demand create karna jo naturally exist nahi karti thi, matlab log pehle us product ke baare me soch bhi nahi rahe the lekin aapne unke dimaag me ek nayi zarurat create kar di, jaise ek time tha jab log normal chips khakar hi khush the, lekin jab Balaji Chips ne apni strong branding aur aggressive distribution ke through market me entry ki to unhone sirf chips nahi becha, balki ek habit create ki, unhone local level par itna strong network banaya ki har chhoti dukaan par unka product available ho gaya aur dheere dheere logon ko lagne laga ki Balaji Chips ek trusted aur better option hai, yahan par demand naturally nahi thi, usko smart strategy se create kiya gaya.

Isi tarah se jab aap koi naya product launch karte hain to aapko ye sochna hota hai ki log abhi kya use kar rahe hain aur aap unhe kaise convince kar sakte hain ki aapka product unse better hai, example ke liye agar aap ek online course bana rahe hain jo Amazon selling sikhata hai to aap directly ye nahi bolte ki "mera course kharido", balki aap pehle logon ko ye realize karvate ho ki job ke alawa bhi income ke sources hone chahiye aur online earning ek powerful option hai, phir aap unhe dikhate ho ki Amazon ek trusted platform hai jahan se log lakho kama rahe hain, aur finally aap apne course ko ek bridge ke roop me present karte ho jo unhe beginner se expert bana sakta hai, yahan aapne pehle demand create ki aur phir product introduce kiya.

Ab baat karte hain “Curiosity Marketing” ki, jo demand create karne ka sabse powerful tareeka hai, curiosity ka matlab hota hai logon ke dimaag me ek aisa sawaal paida kar dena jiska answer wo jaana chahte hain, jab insaan curious hota hai to wo automatically us cheez ke baare me aur jaanne ki koshish karta hai, aur yahi point hota hai jahan se aap usko apne funnel me le aate ho, jaise agar aap simple post karte ho “mera course buy karo” to koi interest nahi lega, lekin agar aap likhte ho “kaise ek student ne sirf 30 din me Amazon se apni pehli earning ki bina kisi investment ke” to yahan ek curiosity create hoti hai aur log click karte hain, ye hi curiosity marketing ka power hai.

Curiosity marketing ka use har jagah hota hai, YouTube thumbnails se lekar Instagram reels tak, sab jagah creators aise titles aur visuals use karte hain jo aadmi ko rok de aur soche “ye kya hai”, jaise “90% log ye mistake karte hain jab wo online earning start karte hain” ya “ye ek secret trick aapki sales double kar sakti hai”, ye sab lines curiosity trigger karti hain aur user ko engage karti hain, jab wo engage hota hai tab aap usko value dete ho aur dheere dheere usko buyer me convert karte ho.

Demand create karne ka ek aur important element hai "Social Proof", jab log dekhte hain ki dusre log bhi kisi product ko use kar rahe hain aur unhe benefit mil raha hai to unka trust automatically badh jata hai, jaise agar aap kisi restaurant ke bahar lambi line dekhte ho to aapko lagta hai ki yahan ka khana accha hoga, waise hi online world me reviews, testimonials aur case studies demand ko boost karte hain, example ke liye agar aap apne course ke saath real students ke results dikhate ho jinhone earning start ki hai to naye logon ko bhi confidence aata hai ki ye kaam karega.

Ab ek aur powerful strategy hai "Scarcity aur Urgency", jab kisi cheez ki availability limited hoti hai to uski demand automatically badh jati hai, jaise "sirf 100 seats available" ya "offer sirf 24 hours ke liye valid hai", ye lines customer ko fast decision lene ke liye push karti hain kyunki unhe lagta hai ki agar abhi nahi liya to baad me chance nahi milega, lekin is strategy ka use genuine hona chahiye warna trust break ho sakta hai.

Demand create karne ke liye aapko apne audience ke emotions ko samajhna padta hai, kyunki log logical reasons se kam aur emotional reasons se zyada kharidte hain, jaise koi fitness product sirf muscles ke liye nahi bikta balki confidence aur attractive look ke liye bikta hai, koi course sirf knowledge ke liye nahi bikta balki better future aur financial freedom ke liye bikta hai, jab aap apne product ko emotion ke saath connect kar dete ho tab demand naturally build hoti hai.

Ek aur important concept hai “Positioning”, matlab aap apne product ko market me kis tarah present kar rahe ho, agar aap apne product ko cheap aur average dikhate ho to log usko seriously nahi lenge, lekin agar aap usko premium aur valuable dikhate ho to log usko ek opportunity ke roop me dekhenge, jaise Apple apne products ko sirf phone ke roop me nahi balki ek status symbol ke roop me present karta hai, isi wajah se log uske liye premium price dene ko ready hote hain.

Finally, demand create karna ek continuous process hai, ye ek baar ka kaam nahi hai, aapko consistently apne audience ke saath engage rehna padta hai, unhe educate karna padta hai, unhe inspire karna padta hai aur unhe dikhana padta hai ki aapka product unki life me kaise difference la sakta hai, jab aap ye sab sahi tarike se karte ho to selling automatic ho jati hai, aapko push nahi karna padta balki log khud aapke paas aate hain aur kehte hain “mujhe ye chahiye”.

Is chapter ka core lesson simple hai lekin powerful hai — “Pehle logon ke dimaag me demand paida karo, phir product becho”, agar aapne ye skill master kar li to aap kisi bhi market me apni jagah bana sakte ho aur apne business ko next level tak le ja sakte ho.

6

Local Marketing Strategies

Marketing ki duniya me ek bahut powerful concept hota hai — *local marketing*. Bahut log sochte hain ki bada business karne ke liye online jana zaroori hai, ads chalana zaroori hai, ya lakho rupaye invest karna zaroori hai, lekin sach ye hai ki agar aap apne local area ko samajh gaye, to aap bina bade budget ke bhi apna business successful bana sakte hain, kyunki har business ki shuruaat hamesha chhote level se hoti hai aur wahi se strong foundation banta hai.

Local marketing ka simple matlab hai apne aas-paas ke logon ko target karna, unki needs samajhna aur unhe apna product ya service sell karna, kyunki ye log aapke sabse pehle aur sabse reliable customers hote hain, aur agar ye satisfied ho gaye to ye hi aapke liye free marketing bhi karte hain.

Sabse pehla aur sabse important factor hota hai **shop location**. Bahut log is cheez ko ignore kar dete hain aur bas rent kam dekh kar kahi bhi shop khol lete hain, lekin location hi decide karti hai ki aapke paas kitne log aayenge, kyunki agar aapki shop aisi jagah par hai jahan log already aate-jate hain, to aapko customers lane ke liye alag se zyada effort nahi karna padega, jaise agar koi person fast food ka stall kisi busy market, school ke paas ya bus stand ke paas lagata hai, to naturally uske paas zyada customers aayenge, wahi agar wo same stall kisi sunsaan gali me laga de to chahe uska khana kitna bhi tasty ho, logon tak pahunch hi nahi payega.

Yahan ek simple sa real example samajhiye — agar koi chai bechne wala apni shop railway station ke bahar lagata hai, to uske paas har waqt log aayenge kyunki wahan crowd already present hota hai, lekin agar wahi chai wala kisi aise area me shop kholta hai jahan log kam aate hain, to usse customers lane ke liye extra marketing karni padegi, isliye location ek silent salesman ki tarah kaam karta hai jo bina bole aapke liye customers laata hai.

Ab baat karte hain dusre powerful strategy ki — **free sample**. Ye ek aisi technique hai jo directly customer ke mind par impact karti hai, kyunki jab tak log kisi product ko try nahi karte, tab tak wo us par trust nahi karte, aur trust ke bina sale hona mushkil hota hai, lekin jaise hi aap unhe free me thoda sa taste ya experience dete hain, unka doubt khatam ho jata hai aur wo khud decide kar lete hain ki product lena hai ya nahi.

Isko ek real life situation se samajhiye — jab aap kisi mall ya market me jate hain aur koi aapko free me biscuit ya juice taste karne deta hai, to aap bina soche try kar lete hain aur agar taste accha lagta hai to aap us product ko kharidne ke chances bahut zyada badh jate hain, isi tarah agar koi naya snacks brand apne chips ka free sample logon ko deta hai, to log usse try karenge aur agar unhe pasand aaya to wo usse kharidna shuru kar denge.

Free sample sirf food industry me hi nahi balki har type ke business me kaam karta hai, jaise agar koi coaching institute first class free de deta hai, ya koi gym ek din ka free trial de deta hai, to log bina risk ke try karte hain aur agar unhe value milti hai to wo paid customer ban jate hain, isliye free sample ek investment hota hai jo future me profit laata hai.

Ab aate hain teesre concept par — **crowd psychology**. Ye concept samajhna thoda interesting hai, kyunki insaan aksar wahi karta hai jo dusre log kar rahe hote hain, matlab agar kisi jagah par bheed lagi hoti hai, to automatically naye log bhi attract hote hain aur sochte hain ki “yahan kuch accha hi mil raha hoga”.

Isko ek simple example se samajhiye — agar aap kisi market me jate hain aur wahan do food stalls lage hote hain, ek stall bilkul khaali hota hai aur dusre stall par bahut bheed hoti hai, to aap naturally kis stall par jayenge? Zyada chances hain ki aap bheed wale stall par hi jayenge, kyunki aapke mind me ye belief ban jata hai ki jahan zyada log hain, wahan product accha hoga, aur ye hi crowd psychology ka magic hai.

Smart business owners is concept ko use karte hain, jaise kuch log starting me apne friends ya relatives ko shop par bula kar thodi bheed create kar dete hain, taki real customers attract ho sake, ya phir kuch brands apne shop ke bahar limited stock ka board laga dete hain taki logon ko lage ki demand zyada hai aur wo jaldi se product kharid lein.

Ab baat karte hain last aur sabse powerful strategy ki — **offer strategy**. Offers ka naam sunte hi har customer ka attention automatically attract ho jata hai, kyunki insaan naturally deals aur discounts ki taraf attract hota hai, lekin yahan samajhne wali baat ye hai ki sirf discount dena hi offer strategy nahi hota, balki smart tarike se offer design karna hi asli game hai.

Jaise agar aap simple 10% discount dete hain, to ho sakta hai log utna excite na ho, lekin agar aap "Buy 1 Get 1 Free" ka offer dete hain, to log usse zyada valuable samajhte hain, chahe dono ka actual value same hi kyu na ho, isi tarah agar aap limited time offer dete hain jaise "sirf aaj ke liye" ya "first 50 customers ke liye", to log jaldi decision lete hain kyunki unhe lagta hai ki agar abhi nahi liya to baad me chance nahi milega.

Ek real example dekhiye — agar koi clothing shop festival ke time par "Flat 50% Off" ka banner lagati hai, to log wahan attract hote hain aur shopping karne ke chances badh jate hain, ya agar koi restaurant "Combo Offer" deta hai jisme burger, fries aur drink ek saath saste me milta hai, to log us combo ko lena prefer karte hain kyunki unhe lagta hai ki wo zyada value le rahe hain.

Offer strategy ka ek aur powerful part hota hai urgency create karna, jaise countdown timer ya limited stock show karna, ye sab customer ke mind me fear create karta hai ki agar abhi nahi liya to miss ho jayega, aur isi fear ki wajah se wo jaldi purchase decision le leta hai.

Agar aap in chaaro strategies — shop location, free sample, crowd psychology aur offer strategy — ko ek saath use karte hain, to aapka local business bahut fast grow kar sakta hai, kyunki aap ek taraf sahi jagah par present hain, dusri taraf logon ko try karne ka chance de rahe hain, teesri taraf bheed ka effect create kar rahe hain aur chauthi taraf attractive offers se unhe purchase ke liye push kar rahe hain.

End me bas itna samajh lijiye ki local marketing koi chhoti cheez nahi hai, balki ye ek strong foundation hai jiske upar bada business khada hota hai, aur jo log apne local market ko master kar lete hain, wo future me bade level par bhi easily grow kar sakte hain, kyunki unhe already pata hota hai ki customer kaise sochta hai aur kaise decision leta hai

.

7

Product Presentation & Packaging

Marketing ki duniya me ek bahut hi powerful truth hai jo beginners aksar ignore kar dete hain: *log pehle product ko nahi, uski presentation ko dekhkar decision lete hain.* Matlab aapka product kitna bhi achha kyu na ho, agar uski packaging aur presentation weak hai, to customer usse seriously nahi lega. Is chapter ka core concept ye hai ki *"jo dikhta hai, wahi bikta hai"* — aur ye sirf ek dialogue nahi, balki real market reality hai. Sabse pehle samajhte hain ki **Product Presentation kya hoti hai**. Simple language me, product presentation ka matlab hota hai ki aap apne product ko customer ke saamne kaise dikhate hain — chahe wo physical store me ho ya online platform par. Isme product ka look, feel, arrangement, lighting, description, aur overall appearance sab include hota hai. Example ke liye agar aap ek same quality ka chocolate lete hain, ek simple transparent polythene me aur dusra ek premium box me golden wrapping ke saath, to naturally aap dusre wale ko zyada value denge, kyunki uski presentation strong hai.

Yahan ek important psychology ka concept kaam karta hai jise bolte hain **"First Impression Bias"** — customer pehla impression dekhkar hi product ki quality judge kar leta hai, jaise agar ek local shop par biscuits khule dabbe me rakhe ho aur ek dusri shop par wahi biscuits neatly packed aur shelf me arranged ho, to customer automatically dusri shop ko zyada trust karega.

Ab baat karte hain **Packaging ki**, jo presentation ka sabse important part hai. Packaging sirf product ko cover karne ke liye nahi hoti, balki wo ek silent salesman hoti hai jo bina bole customer ko convince karti hai. Ek achhi packaging teen kaam karti hai: *protect karti hai, attract karti hai, aur communicate karti hai.* Protect ka matlab product safe rahe, attract ka matlab customer ka attention grab kare, aur communicate ka matlab product ki value aur brand message clear kare.

Example samajhiye: agar aap roadside se ek juice lete hain jo simple glass me diya jata hai aur dusri taraf ek branded tetra pack juice lete hain jisme proper labeling, design aur information hoti hai, to aap second option ko zyada safe aur premium maanenge, chahe taste similar hi kyu na ho.

Ab samajhte hain **Attractive Packaging ka concept**. Attractive packaging ka matlab sirf colorful hona nahi hota, balki wo customer ke emotion aur expectation ke saath match hona chahiye. Jaise agar aap kids ke liye product bana rahe hain, to bright colors, cartoon characters aur fun design use karna effective hoga, wahi agar aap luxury product sell kar rahe hain to minimal design, dark colors aur premium finish zyada impactful hota hai.

Yahan ek real-life pattern hai: *log packaging dekhkar hi product ki price guess karte hain,* jaise agar ek perfume simple plastic bottle me ho to wo cheap lagega, lekin agar wahi perfume glass bottle me aur elegant box ke saath ho to wo premium feel dega aur log uske liye zyada paisa dene ko ready ho jate hain.

Iske baad aata hai **Product Display**, jo especially offline stores aur online listings dono me important role play karta hai. Product display ka matlab hota hai ki aap apne product ko kaise arrange karte hain taki wo easily visible aur appealing lage. Ek smart display customer ki attention ko guide karta hai aur unhe purchase decision lene me help karta hai.

Example ke liye agar ek clothing store me kapde random tarike se pile up ho, aur dusre store me same kapde color-wise aur category-wise arranged ho, to customer dusre store me zyada comfortable feel karega aur zyada time spend karega, jisse sales badhne ke chances automatically increase ho jate hain.

Online world me bhi display utna hi important hai. Agar aap Amazon ya kisi bhi e-commerce platform par sell karte hain, to aapki product image, background, angle, lighting, aur description hi aapka display hai. Example ke liye agar ek product ki image blurry ho aur dusre ki high-quality clear image ho with multiple angles, to customer naturally second option choose karega.

Ab aate hain **Branding Importance par**, jo packaging aur presentation dono ka backbone hai. Branding ka matlab hota hai aapke product ki identity — jo aapko dusre competitors se alag banati hai. Branding sirf logo tak limited nahi hoti, balki usme aapka color scheme, font style, packaging design, messaging aur overall vibe include hota hai.

Ek strong brand ka fayda ye hota hai ki customer aapke product ko pehchanne lagta hai aur trust develop karta hai, jaise agar koi customer ek baar kisi brand ka biscuit kharidta hai aur uska experience acha hota hai, to next time wo same brand ka product bina soche kharid lega, even agar thoda mehenga ho.

Yahan ek important concept hai **"Perceived Value"** — iska matlab hota hai ki customer product ki actual value nahi, balki uski perceived value ke hisaab se paisa deta hai, jaise agar ek water bottle simple ho to wo ₹20 me bikti hai, lekin agar wahi bottle premium packaging aur branding ke saath aaye to wo ₹50 ya usse zyada me bhi sell ho sakti hai.

Packaging aur branding ka ek hidden benefit ye bhi hai ki wo **word-of-mouth marketing** ko boost karta hai, jaise agar aap kisi ko ek beautifully packed gift dete hain, to wo sirf product hi nahi, balki uski packaging bhi notice karta hai aur dusron ko batata hai, is tarah aapka brand organically grow karta hai.

Ab ek aur practical angle samajhte hain — **Consistency**. Aapki packaging aur presentation har jagah consistent honi chahiye, chahe wo offline store ho, online listing ho ya social media. Agar aapka brand ek jagah premium lag raha hai aur dusri jagah cheap, to customer confuse ho jayega aur trust kam ho jayega.

Example ke liye agar aap Instagram par apne product ko luxury brand ke jaise present karte hain lekin delivery ke time product simple plastic me aaye, to customer disappointed hoga aur repeat purchase ke chances kam ho jayenge.

Isliye ek smart business owner hamesha ye ensure karta hai ki *customer ka experience start se end tak consistent aur satisfying ho.*

Ab baat karte hain ek powerful strategy ki jise bolte hain **"Unboxing Experience"**. Aaj ke time me sirf product sell karna enough nahi hai, balki customer ko ek memorable experience dena important hai. Jab customer product open karta hai aur usse ek premium feel aata hai, to wo emotionally connect ho jata hai.

Example ke liye agar aap ek online order receive karte hain jisme neatly packed box, thank you note aur clean arrangement ho, to aap automatically impressed ho jate hain aur brand ke bare me positive sochte hain.

Is chapter ka final aur sabse important lesson ye hai ki *product sirf uski quality se nahi, balki uski presentation, packaging aur branding se bikta hai.* Agar aap in teen cheezon ko master kar lete hain, to aap average product ko bhi successful bana sakte hain, lekin agar aap inhe ignore karte hain to best product bhi fail ho sakta hai.

Isliye hamesha yaad rakhiye: **Customer pehle dekhta hai, fir sochta hai, aur last me kharidta hai — aur aapka kaam hai uske dekhne wale moment ko itna powerful banana ki wo bina hesitation ke buy button dabaa de.**

8

Word of Mouth Marketing

Marketing ki duniya me agar koi ek aisa powerful tool hai jo bina zyada paisa kharch kiye aapke business ko upar le ja sakta hai, to wo hai *Word of Mouth Marketing*. Iska simple matlab hai jab aapke customers khud aapke product ya service ke baare me dusre logon ko batate hain, recommend karte hain, aur unhe kharidne ke liye motivate karte hain. Ye marketing ka sabse natural aur sabse trusted form hota hai, kyunki yahan promotion kisi company ke ad se nahi, balki ek real insaan ke experience se aata hai, aur log ads se zyada apne friends, family ya jaan-pehchaan ke logon ki baat par trust karte hain.

Sabse pehle samajhte hain ki Word of Mouth itna powerful kyu hota hai. Jab koi company khud apne product ki tarif karti hai, to log usse marketing samajhte hain, lekin jab koi customer bina kisi fayde ke khud kisi product ki tarif karta hai, to wo ek honest opinion lagta hai, aur wahi trust create karta hai. Example ke liye agar aapka dost aapko bolta hai ki "bhai ye wali chai ki dukaan best hai, taste bhi mast hai

aur price bhi sahi hai", to aap us dukaan ko try karne ke chances zyada hote hain, kyunki wo recommendation kisi ad se nahi balki ek real experience se aa rahi hai.
Word of Mouth Marketing ka base hota hai *customer satisfaction*, yani agar aapka customer khush hai, tabhi wo aapke baare me dusron ko batayega. Agar aapka product average hai, ya service me problem hai, to log ya to chup rehte hain ya phir negative baat failate hain, aur negative word of mouth positive se bhi zyada fast spread hota hai. Isliye sabse pehla rule ye hai ki aap apne customer ko itna satisfy karo ki wo naturally aapka promoter ban jaye. Customer satisfaction ka matlab sirf product bech dena nahi hota, balki pura experience hota hai. Isme product quality, packaging, behavior, service, delivery sab include hota hai. Example ke liye agar aap ek small bakery chalate hain aur aapka cake taste me acha hai, lekin staff rude hai, to customer ka overall experience kharab ho jayega aur wo recommend nahi karega, lekin agar cake acha ho, packaging attractive ho aur staff polite ho to customer khud bolega "yahan ka cake try karo, bahut acha hai".
Ab aate hain *referral* par, jo Word of Mouth ka ek structured version hai. Referral ka matlab hai jab aap apne existing customers ko motivate karte hain ki wo naye customers lekar aayein, aur uske badle me unhe koi reward mile. Ye ek smart strategy hai jisme aap apne satisfied customers ko apne marketing partner bana dete hain. Example ke liye agar aap ek gym chalate hain aur aap bolte

hain "agar aap apne friend ko join karwate ho to aapko 1 month free milega", to aapka current customer apne doston ko invite karega, kyunki usse bhi benefit mil raha hai. Referral ka sabse bada benefit ye hai ki yahan trust already built hota hai, kyunki jo naya customer aa raha hai wo kisi known person ki recommendation par aa raha hai. Isliye referral se aaye hue customers ka conversion rate aur retention dono high hota hai. Lekin referral tabhi kaam karta hai jab aapka product ya service genuinely acha ho, warna koi bhi apne friend ko recommend nahi karega.

Ab samajhte hain *local reputation* ke baare me, jo Word of Mouth ka ek aur important part hai. Local business ke liye reputation sab kuch hota hai, kyunki yahan log ek dusre se directly influence hote hain. Agar aapki dukaan ya service kisi area me famous ho gayi, to log bina soche samjhe aapke paas aayenge, aur agar aapki reputation kharab ho gayi, to log avoid karenge. Example ke liye agar kisi area me ek barber shop famous ho jaye ki wahan haircut perfect hota hai, to log thoda door se bhi wahan aayenge, lekin agar ek baar logon ko lage ki wahan service kharab hai, to word spread hone me time nahi lagega.

Word of Mouth Marketing ko strong banane ke liye aapko kuch important principles follow karne hote hain. Sabse pehla principle hai *expectation se zyada dena*. Agar customer jo expect kar raha hai aap usse thoda extra dete hain, to wo impress hota hai aur share karta hai. Example ke liye agar koi customer ek product order karta hai aur uske saath aap ek small free gift ya thank you note bhejte hain, to uska experience memorable ban jata hai aur wo dusron ko batata hai.

Dusra principle hai *consistency*, yani har customer ko same quality aur experience milna chahiye. Agar kabhi acha aur kabhi kharab experience mila, to log confused ho jate hain aur recommend nahi karte. Word of Mouth tabhi grow karta hai jab logon ko pata hota hai ki yahan hamesha acha hi milega.

Teesra principle hai *emotion create karna*. Log facts nahi, feelings share karte hain. Agar aapka product ya service kisi ko khush, excited ya special feel karata hai, to wo automatically share karta hai. Example ke liye agar aap ek restaurant chalate hain aur aap birthday par customer ko surprise cake de dete hain, to wo moment itna special hota hai ki wo social media par share hota hai aur dusre log attract hote hain.

Ab ek important baat samajhni hai ki Word of Mouth sirf offline nahi hota, online bhi hota hai. Aaj ke time me log reviews, ratings aur social media posts ke through bhi apne experience share karte hain. Agar kisi product ke ache reviews hain, to naye customers attract hote hain, aur agar negative reviews zyada hain, to log avoid karte hain. Isliye aapko apne customers ko encourage karna chahiye ki wo feedback dein, review likhein aur apna experience share karein.

Negative Word of Mouth se bhi bachna bahut zaroori hai. Agar koi customer unhappy hai, to usse ignore karne ke bajay uski problem solve karni chahiye, kyunki ek unhappy customer 10 logon ko bata sakta hai, jabki ek happy customer shayad 3–4 logon ko batata hai. Example ke liye agar kisi customer ko product me defect mil gaya aur aap turant replace kar dete hain aur politely handle karte hain, to wo negative experience positive me convert ho sakta hai aur wo aapki honesty ko appreciate karega.

Word of Mouth Marketing ko boost karne ke liye aapko apne customers ke saath relationship build karna hota hai, sirf transaction nahi. Jab customer ko lagta hai ki aap uski value karte hain, uski respect karte hain aur uska khayal rakhte hain, to wo aapke brand se emotionally connect ho jata hai, aur wahi connection usse dusron ko recommend karne ke liye motivate karta hai.

End me simple si baat ye hai ki Word of Mouth Marketing koi shortcut nahi hai, ye ek result hai jo aapko tab milta hai jab aap genuinely acha product aur service dete hain, apne customers ko happy rakhte hain aur unhe ek memorable experience dete hain. Agar aapka focus sirf bechne par hai to Word of Mouth nahi banega, lekin agar aapka focus customer ko khush karne par hai to Word of Mouth automatically generate hoga.

Is chapter ka core lesson ye hai ki “best marketing wo hoti hai jo aapke customers khud aapke liye karte hain”, isliye apne business ko is tarah build karo ki har customer aapka brand ambassador ban jaye, kyunki jab log aapke baare me baat karna start kar dete hain, tab aapko marketing push nahi karni padti, market khud aapko push karta hai.

9

Social Media Marketing

Digital duniya ne business ka pura game hi change kar diya hai, aur aaj ke time me agar aap social media ka sahi use nahi kar rahe ho, to aap apne business ke sabse bade opportunity ko miss kar rahe ho. Social Media Marketing sirf post dalne ka naam nahi hai, balki ye ek powerful system hai jisme aap apne customer ke saath connection banate ho, trust create karte ho, aur dheere-dheere unhe buyer me convert karte ho. Is chapter me hum bilkul basic se samjhenge ki Social Media Marketing kaise kaam karta hai aur kaise aap ise use karke apna business grow kar sakte ho.

Sabse pehle samajhte hain ki Social Media Marketing hota kya hai. Simple language me bole to, jab aap kisi bhi social platform par apne product ya service ko promote karte ho, apni audience se interact karte ho aur unhe engage karte ho, use Social Media Marketing kehte hain. Yaha par sirf bechna hi goal nahi hota, balki relationship banana sabse important hota hai. Kyunki social media par log ads dekhne nahi, balki content consume karne aate hain.

Aaj ke time me sabse powerful platforms me se ek hai Instagram. Instagram ek visual platform hai jahan photo, video aur reels ke through aap apni story bata sakte ho. Instagram marketing ka basic funda hai “Attention grab karo aur interest build karo”. Jab koi user scroll kar raha hota hai, to uska attention sirf 2-3 second ke liye hi hota hai, agar aapka content us time me usko attract nahi karta, to wo aage badh jata hai.

Instagram par marketing karne ke liye sabse pehla step hota hai apna profile setup karna. Aapka profile hi aapka digital shop hai, jahan log aake decide karte hain ki aap trustworthy ho ya nahi. Profile picture clear hona chahiye, bio me simple aur clear likha hona chahiye ki aap kya offer karte ho, aur aapke highlights me aapke products ya services ka demo hona chahiye, example ke liye agar koi local कपड़ों की दुकान wala apne Instagram par daily naye design ki reels dalta hai aur bio me “Latest Fashion at Affordable Price” likhta hai, to jo bhi user uska profile dekhega usko turant samajh aa jayega ki ye page kis bare me hai.

Instagram me content sabse bada king hota hai. Aap jitna valuable aur interesting content doge, utna hi aap grow karoge. Content teen type ka hota hai – educational, entertaining aur promotional. Educational content me aap logon ko kuch sikhate ho, entertaining me unhe entertain karte ho aur promotional me apna product sell karte ho, example ke liye agar aap shoes bechte ho to aap ek reel bana sakte ho jisme aap “5 mistakes while buying shoes” batate ho, isse log aapse connect karte hain aur end me aap apna product show karte ho.

Ab baat karte hain reels ki, jo aaj ke time me Instagram ka sabse powerful feature hai. Short videos jaldi viral hote hain aur aapko organic reach dete hain. Reels me aapko storytelling aur trending music ka use karna chahiye, example ke liye ek small food stall owner apne stall ka behind-the-scenes video banata hai jisme wo dikhata hai ki wo kaise fresh samosa bana raha hai, ye video logon ko attract karta hai aur wo us stall par visit karne lagte hain.

Instagram marketing me consistency bhi bahut important hai. Aapko regular post karna hota hai, kyunki algorithm unhi accounts ko promote karta hai jo active rehte hain. Agar aap 2 din post karke 10 din break le loge, to aapka growth ruk jayega.

Ab chalte hain dusre powerful platform par, jo har Indian ke phone me hota hai, wo hai WhatsApp. WhatsApp Marketing ek aisa tool hai jahan aap directly apne customer ke inbox me ja sakte ho, aur ye sabse personal aur direct marketing ka form hai. Yaha par aapka connection already strong hota hai kyunki jo bhi aapke contact me hai wo aapko jaanta hai ya aapka number save kiya hua hai.

WhatsApp marketing ka sabse basic use hota hai broadcast aur groups. Broadcast me aap ek message ek saath multiple logon ko bhej sakte ho bina group banaye, example ke liye agar aap ek bakery owner ho aur aapne naya cake introduce kiya hai to aap apne customers ko ek attractive image ke saath message bhej sakte ho “Fresh Chocolate Cake Available Today, Order Now”, isse direct orders aane lagte hain.

WhatsApp Status bhi ek underrated tool hai. Aap apne daily updates, offers aur products ko status me dal sakte ho, jo log aapka number save kiye hue hain wo daily aapka status dekhte hain, example ke liye ek mobile shop owner daily apne shop ke new arrivals ka status dalta hai aur log directly usko message karke price puchte hain aur order place kar dete hain.

WhatsApp marketing me sabse important hota hai trust aur personalization. Yaha par aap spam nahi kar sakte, agar aap baar-baar irrelevant message bhejoge to log aapko block kar denge. Isliye hamesha useful aur relevant content hi share karein, example ke liye agar aap coaching center chalate ho to aap students ko daily ek useful tip ya question bhej sakte ho, jisse wo aapke saath engaged rahenge.

Ab baat karte hain teesre aur sabse fast growing method ki, jo hai short video marketing. Aaj ke time me log lambi videos ya articles kam dekhte hain, wo short aur engaging content prefer karte hain. Short video platforms jaise Instagram Reels, YouTube Shorts aur dusre apps ne marketing ka pura trend hi badal diya hai.

Short video marketing ka main funda hai “कम समय में ज्यादा value देना”. Aapko 15-30 second ke andar hi apna message deliver karna hota hai. Isme aapko hook, content aur call to action ka use karna hota hai. Hook matlab starting me kuch aisa bolna ya dikhana jo attention grab kare, content me aap value dete ho aur end me call to action dete ho jaise “Follow for more” ya “DM to order”.

Short video marketing me authenticity sabse important hoti hai. Log polished ads se jyada real aur raw content ko pasand karte hain, example ke liye ek small farmer apne organic vegetables ka video banata hai jisme wo apne farm dikhata hai aur batata hai ki wo bina chemicals ke sabzi ugata hai, ye video logon ko trust dilata hai aur wo directly usse purchase karte hain.

Ek aur important cheez hai trend ka use karna. Agar koi audio ya style viral ho raha hai, to aap usko apne content me use kar sakte ho. Ye aapki reach ko increase karta hai, example ke liye agar koi trending dialogue chal raha hai to aap us dialogue ke saath apne product ko creatively show kar sakte ho.

Ab sabse important baat ye hai ki in tino platforms ko alag-alag nahi balki ek system ki tarah use karna chahiye. Instagram se aap audience attract karte ho, WhatsApp se aap unhe convert karte ho aur short videos se aap apni reach badhate ho, example ke liye ek clothing seller Instagram par reels dalta hai jisme wo apne latest collection dikhata hai aur caption me likhta hai “For order DM or

WhatsApp", fir jo log interested hote hain wo WhatsApp par aate hain aur waha se wo order place kar dete hain.
Social Media Marketing me patience bhi bahut zaruri hai. Ye ek din me result dene wala system nahi hai, aapko time dena padta hai, consistency maintain karni padti hai aur continuously improve karna padta hai. Jo log jaldi give up kar dete hain, wo kabhi success nahi dekh pate.
Aakhir me ek simple sa rule yaad rakhiye, "People don't buy products, they buy trust". Agar aap social media par trust build kar loge, to aap kuch bhi sell kar sakte ho. Aapka goal sirf bechna nahi hona chahiye, balki logon ki problem solve karna hona chahiye, jab aap genuinely logon ki help karoge, to wo automatically aapke customer ban jayenge.
Is tarah Social Media Marketing ek powerful tool hai jo aapko zero se hero bana sakta hai, bas aapko ise sahi tarike se samajhna aur apply karna hai.

10

Sales Funnel Strategy

Business ko grow karne ka sabse powerful aur practical system agar koi hai, to wo hai **Sales Funnel**. Bahut log direct sale karne ki galti karte hain, matlab wo apna product dekhte hi customer ko bol dete hain "buy now", lekin reality ye hai ki koi bhi insan bina soche samjhe turant paisa spend nahi karta, wo pehle aapko notice karta hai, fir interest develop hota hai, fir trust banta hai aur uske baad hi wo purchase decision leta hai. Isi pure process ko systematically samajhna aur apply karna hi Sales Funnel Strategy kehlata hai.

Simple words me samjhein to Sales Funnel ek journey hai jo ek unknown person ko step-by-step aapka customer banati hai, aur is journey ke 4 main stages hote hain: **Attention → Interest → Trust → Sale**.

Sabse pehla step hota hai **Attention**. Is stage ka main goal hota hai logon ka dhyaan apni taraf attract karna, kyunki jab tak log aapko notice hi nahi karenge tab tak aap unhe kuch sell nahi kar sakte. Aaj ke time me attention sabse mehengi cheez hai kyunki har jagah competition hai, har koi ads chala raha hai, reels bana raha hai, offers de raha hai, isliye aapko kuch aisa karna padega jo logon ko rukne par majboor kare. Attention create karne ke liye aap social media posts, short videos, ads, catchy headlines, ya unique content ka use kar sakte hain, jaise ek online seller agar Instagram par ek reel banata hai jisme wo dikhata hai "sirf ₹50 me profitable product kaise find kare Amazon par" to ye line turant logon ka attention grab karti hai kyunki ye unki curiosity ko trigger karti hai.

Yahan ek important baat samajhni hai ki attention ka matlab sirf views lana nahi hota, balki **right audience ka attention lana** hota hai, agar aapke content ko 1 lakh log dekh rahe hain lekin unme se koi bhi aapka potential customer nahi hai to wo useless hai, lekin agar 1000 sahi log dekh rahe hain jo aapke product me interested ho sakte hain to wo zyada valuable hai. Isliye attention stage me clarity hona bahut zaroori hai ki aap kis type ke logon ko attract karna chahte hain.

Ab aata hai second stage **Interest**. Jab kisi ka attention aap par aa jata hai to agla step hota hai us interest ko develop karna, matlab ab aapko unhe engage karna hai, unhe batana hai ki aapka product ya service unke liye kyu useful hai. Yahan par aapko sirf selling nahi karni balki value deni hoti hai, jaise informative content, tips, tricks, problem solving videos, ya educational posts ke through aap logon ko apne saath jodte hain, jaise agar aap Amazon selling sikhate hain to aap ek reel me batate hain “3 mistakes jo new sellers Amazon par karte hain aur kaise avoid kare” to jo log already Amazon me interested hain wo aapko follow karna start karenge kyunki unhe lagta hai ki aap unki problem solve kar sakte hain.

Interest stage me sabse bada kaam hota hai logon ko apne ecosystem me lana, jaise Instagram followers banana, WhatsApp group join karwana, email list collect karna ya YouTube subscribers badhana, kyunki jab tak wo aapse connected nahi honge tab tak aap unhe next stage me nahi le ja sakte. Yahan par consistency bahut important hoti hai, ek baar content dal kar chhod dene se interest build nahi hota, aapko regular value deni padti hai.

Teesra stage hota hai **Trust**, aur ye sabse critical stage hota hai, kyunki bina trust ke koi bhi sale possible nahi hai. Aaj ke time me log bahut smart ho gaye hain, wo kisi bhi unknown person se turant product nahi kharidte, wo pehle dekhte hain ki aap genuine ho ya nahi, aapke paas real knowledge hai ya nahi, aur kya dusre log bhi aapse satisfied hain ya nahi. Trust build karne ke liye aapko transparency dikhani hoti hai, apni journey share karni hoti hai, apne results dikhane hote hain, customer testimonials share karne hote hain, aur sabse important consistent value deni hoti hai.

Jaise ek example me samjhein, agar koi person daily apne Instagram par Amazon selling ke tips share karta hai, apne students ke results dikhata hai “mere student ne 30 din me ₹20,000 profit kiya”, apni mistakes aur learnings openly batata hai, to dheere dheere audience ko us par trust hone lagta hai, aur jab trust build ho jata hai to log khud hi uske paid course ya service ke baare me poochne lagte hain. Trust ek din me nahi banta, ye time leta hai, lekin jab ban jata hai to sale automatic ho jati hai.

Ab aata hai last stage **Sale**. Ye wo point hai jahan aap actual me apna product ya service sell karte hain, lekin agar aapne pehle ke teen stages sahi tarike se follow kiye hain to yahan aapko zyada push karne ki zaroorat nahi padti. Sale stage me aapko clear offer dena hota hai, simple language me batana hota hai ki aap kya de rahe hain, kitne me de rahe hain aur customer ko kya benefit milega. Yahan par urgency aur scarcity ka bhi use hota hai jaise “limited seats available”, “offer sirf 3 din ke liye valid hai”, kyunki ye logon ko decision lene ke liye motivate karta hai.

Ek simple real-life flow samjhein to maan lijiye aap ek beginner ke liye Amazon selling course sell kar rahe hain, to pehle aap Instagram par reels bana kar logon ka attention grab karte hain jaise “₹5000 se Amazon business start kaise kare”, fir aap unhe interest me convert karte hain daily useful content dekar jaise product research tips aur common mistakes, fir aap trust build karte hain apne results, student testimonials aur apni journey share karke, aur finally aap ek structured offer dete hain “mera complete Amazon course join kare jisme step-by-step guidance

milega", to jo log pehle se aapko follow kar rahe hain aur trust karte hain wo easily purchase kar lete hain.
Yahan ek bahut badi mistake log karte hain ki wo direct sale par jump kar jate hain bina attention, interest aur trust build kiye, aur fir bolte hain ki product nahi bik raha, jabki problem product me nahi hoti balki process me hoti hai.
Sales Funnel ka magic ye hai ki ye selling ko natural bana deta hai, aapko force karne ki zaroorat nahi padti, customer khud ready ho jata hai buy karne ke liye.
Ek aur important baat ye hai ki funnel ek baar bana lene ke baad aap ise automate bhi kar sakte hain, jaise ads ke through traffic lana, landing page par lead collect karna, email sequence ke through trust build karna aur fir automated sale generate karna, isse aapka business scalable ban jata hai aur aap ek system ke through continuous sales generate kar sakte hain.
End me sirf itna samajh lijiye ki Sales Funnel koi complicated cheez nahi hai, ye bas human behavior ko samajhne ka ek structured tarika hai, har insan pehle dekhta hai, fir sochta hai, fir trust karta hai aur fir buy karta hai, agar aap is natural process ko respect karte hue apni marketing strategy banate hain to aapka business long-term me stable aur profitable ban sakta hai, aur agar aap is process ko ignore karte hain to chahe aapka product kitna bhi achha ho wo market me struggle karega.

Isliye hamesha yaad rakhein: **pehle attention lao, fir interest build karo, fir trust kamao aur uske baad sale apne aap hogi.**

11

Psychology Tricks in Marketing

Jab koi insaan kisi product ko kharidne ka decision leta hai, to wo sirf logic se nahi balki emotions aur psychology se bhi heavily influence hota hai. Isi wajah se successful marketing sirf product dikhane tak limited nahi hoti, balki customer ke mind ko samajhne aur us par subtle impact daalne ki art hoti hai. Psychology tricks ka use karke aap kisi bhi normal product ko bhi high demand me la sakte hain, bas aapko pata hona chahiye ki customer ka dimaag kaise kaam karta hai aur kaunse trigger unhe action lene ke liye majboor karte hain.

Sabse pehla concept aata hai **Scarcity**, jiska simple matlab hai kisi cheez ki kami ya limited availability. Human nature aisa hota hai ki jab hume lagta hai ki koi cheez limited hai ya jaldi khatam ho sakti hai, to hum usko zyada valuable samajhne lagte hain. Example ke liye agar kisi shop par likha ho “Only 5 pieces left”, to customer ke mind me turant ek fear create hota hai ki agar abhi nahi liya to baad me nahi milega, aur isi fear ki wajah se wo jaldi decision le leta hai. Scarcity ek powerful psychological trigger hai jo demand ko instantly boost karta hai, chahe product pehle se available hi kyu na ho.

Iske baad aata hai **Urgency**, jo scarcity se thoda different hai lekin equally powerful hai. Urgency ka matlab hai time ka pressure create karna, jaise “Offer valid till tonight” ya “Sale ends in 2 hours”. Jab customer ko lagta hai ki unke paas decision lene ke liye limited time hai, to wo zyada soch-vichar nahi karte aur impulsive decision le lete hain. Example ke liye online shopping apps par countdown timer dikhaya jata hai jisme likha hota hai “Deal ends in 01:59:30”, ye dekhkar customer ko lagta hai ki agar abhi nahi liya to opportunity chali jayegi, aur wo jaldi se purchase kar leta hai. Urgency basically customer ke overthinking process ko bypass karta hai aur unhe fast action lene par majboor karta hai.

Agla concept hai **Social Proof**, jo marketing me sabse zyada commonly use hone wala trick hai. Social proof ka matlab hai log dusron ko dekhkar decision lete hain. Agar kisi product ke bahut saare positive reviews hain ya bahut log use kar rahe hain, to naye customer ka trust automatically badh jata hai. Example ke liye agar aap kisi restaurant ke bahar bheed dekhte hain, to aapko lagta hai ki yahan ka khana acha hoga, isi liye aap bhi wahan jaana prefer karte hain. Isi tarah online platforms par “10,000+ happy customers” ya “4.5 star rating” jaise elements customer ke mind me trust build karte hain. Log aksar ye sochte hain ki jab itne log use kar rahe hain to ye product galat nahi ho sakta, aur isi psychology ka fayda marketers uthate hain.

Ab baat karte hain sabse interesting aur powerful technique ki, jo hai **Storytelling**. Storytelling ka matlab hai product ko sirf ek cheez ke roop me present na karke uske around ek emotional story create karna. Human brain facts se zyada stories ko easily remember karta hai aur unse emotionally connect bhi karta hai. Example ke liye agar aap ek simple soap bech rahe hain aur sirf ye bolte hain ki “ye skin ko clean karta hai”, to shayad itna impact nahi padega, lekin agar aap ek story batate hain ki kaise ek ladki ko skin problems thi aur is soap ne uski life change kar di, to customer us story se emotionally connect karega aur product kharidne ke chances badh jayenge. Storytelling customer ke mind me ek image create karta hai jisme wo khud ko imagine karta hai, aur jab wo apne aap ko us situation me dekhta hai, to buying decision aur strong ho jata hai.

In sab psychology tricks ka main goal hota hai customer ke decision-making process ko influence karna without forcing them. Ek smart marketer kabhi bhi directly “Buy now” nahi bolta, balki wo aisa environment create karta hai jisme customer khud feel kare ki unhe product lena chahiye. Ye subtle influence hi marketing ko powerful banata hai.

Agar aap in concepts ko combine karke use karte hain, to result aur bhi strong ho jata hai. Jaise ek online store par likha ho "Only 3 items left, 5000+ people already bought, offer ends tonight", to yahan scarcity, social proof aur urgency teeno ek saath kaam kar rahe hain, aur customer ke liye resist karna bahut mushkil ho jata hai. Isi tarah agar aap ek story ke through product ko present karte hain aur uske saath real customer reviews add kar dete hain, to trust aur emotional connection dono ek saath build hote hain.

Ek aur important baat ye hai ki in tricks ka use hamesha ethically hona chahiye. Agar aap fake scarcity ya fake reviews use karte hain, to short-term me sales badh sakti hai lekin long-term me brand ki reputation kharab ho jati hai. Customer ek baar trust lose kar deta hai to usse wapas lana bahut mushkil hota hai, isliye psychology ka use smartly aur honestly karna hi best strategy hoti hai.

Aaj ke digital era me jahan competition bahut zyada hai, wahan sirf product ki quality enough nahi hoti, balki aap us product ko kaise present karte hain aur customer ke mind ko kaise influence karte hain, ye zyada matter karta hai. Psychology tricks ek tarah ka shortcut nahi balki ek science hai jise samajhkar aap apni marketing ko next level par le ja sakte hain.

Agar aap ek beginner hain, to sabse pehle in basic concepts ko samajhiye aur chhote level par implement kijiye, jaise apne product listing me limited stock show karna, WhatsApp status me urgency create karna, ya Instagram par customer feedback share karna, dheere dheere aapko samajh aayega ki kaunsa trick aapke audience par sabse zyada effective hai. Experience ke saath aap apni strategy ko aur refine kar sakte hain aur ek strong marketing system build kar sakte hain.

End me ek simple sa rule yaad rakhiye, log products nahi balki feelings aur solutions kharidte hain, aur psychology tricks ka kaam hota hai un feelings ko activate karna. Jab aap customer ke dimaag aur dil dono ko samajhkar marketing karte hain, tabhi aap real success achieve kar pate hain.

12

Marketing Strategies Used by Famous Brands

Marketing ek aisi kala hai jahan sirf product banana kaafi nahi hota, balki us product ko logon ke dimaag aur dil dono me jagah dilani padti hai, aur jab hum duniya ke sabse successful brands jaise Coca-Cola, Apple, Nike, McDonald's, Red Bull aur Balaji Wafers ko deeply study karte hain, to hume ek bahut powerful baat samajh aati hai — "Success kabhi bhi accident nahi hoti, wo ek planned strategy ka result hoti hai", aur is chapter me hum in brands ke history, unke struggles, unke decisions aur unke marketing secrets ko itni detail me samjhenge ki aap apne business me bhi unko practically apply kar sakein.

Sabse pehle baat karte hain Coca-Cola ki, jiska start 1886 me hua tha jab ek pharmacist John Pemberton ne ek simple syrup banaya tha jo ek drink ke roop me becha gaya, lekin

Coca-Cola ki real success uske taste se nahi balki uski branding se aayi, early days me hi Coca-Cola ne samajh liya tha ki agar brand ko long-term me jeetana hai to usko logon ke emotions se jodna hoga, isliye unhone apni marketing ko “happiness”, “togetherness” aur “celebration” ke around build kiya, ek simple real-life example dekhiye ki jab bhi koi festival hota hai ya family gathering hoti hai to log automatically Coke ko include karte hain bina soche samjhe, ye kisi accident se nahi hua balki decades ki consistent advertising ka result hai jahan har ad me smile, friends aur happy moments dikhaye gaye, Coca-Cola ne ek aur powerful strategy use ki “global consistency”, matlab duniya ke kisi bhi country me chale jaiye Coke ka taste aur brand image same milega, isse trust build hota hai aur customer ko confusion nahi hota, aur sabse interesting baat ye hai ki Coca-Cola ne apni product se zyada apni story ko sell kiya, isliye wo ek drink nahi balki ek emotion ban gaya.

Ab agar hum Apple ki baat karein to ye brand marketing ka ek premium example hai jahan product ke saath-saath perception ko sell kiya jata hai, Apple ki journey 1976 me garage se start hui thi lekin aaj wo duniya ke sabse valuable brands me se ek hai, iska main reason hai “Think Different” philosophy jo Apple ne apne core me rakhi, Apple kabhi bhi apne product ko sirf features ke basis par sell nahi karta balki wo creativity, innovation aur status ko sell karta hai, ek simple example dekhiye ki jab koi iPhone kharidta hai to wo sirf phone nahi leta balki ek identity kharidta hai, Apple ki ek bahut powerful strategy hai "minimalism", chahe wo product design ho ya advertising, Apple hamesha simple aur clean messaging use karta hai jisse customer confuse nahi hota aur directly value samajh me aati hai, aur ek aur secret strategy hai "controlled scarcity", Apple apne launches ko limited excitement ke saath release karta hai jisse demand automatically increase ho jati hai, log line me lagte hain kyunki unhe lagta hai ki ye product special hai, aur isi wajah se Apple ne apne aap ko ek luxury brand ke roop me establish kiya.

Ab aate hain Nike par jo ek emotional branding ka king maana jata hai, Nike ka start ek simple sports shoe company ke roop me hua tha lekin aaj wo ek global inspiration brand ban chuka hai, Nike ki sabse powerful strategy hai "storytelling", wo apne ads me product nahi balki struggle aur success ki kahani dikhata hai, ek example dekhiye ki jab koi beginner athlete Nike ka ad dekhta hai jahan ek struggling player hard work karke success pa raha hai to wo emotionally connect ho jata hai aur feel karta hai ki wo bhi kar sakta hai, Nike ne influencers aur athletes ka bhi bahut smart use kiya jisse brand credibility badhi, lekin sabse important baat ye hai ki Nike ne apne brand ko "Just Do It" jaise powerful message ke saath attach kar diya jo har insaan ke andar ke fear ko challenge karta hai, aur isi wajah se Nike sirf sports brand nahi balki ek motivation brand ban gaya.

Ab samajhte hain McDonald's ko jo consistency aur system ka perfect example hai, McDonald's ka start ek small restaurant se hua tha lekin aaj wo global empire ban chuka hai, iska main reason hai "standardization", McDonald's ne ek aisa system create kiya jahan har outlet me same process follow hota hai jisse har jagah same taste aur quality milti hai, ek real example dekhiye ki agar aap India me McDonald's jaate hain ya kisi aur country me, aapko same experience milega, isse customer trust build hota hai aur wo repeat visit karta hai, McDonald's ne "fast service" concept ko bhi popular banaya jisse busy lifestyle wale log easily food le sakein, aur unki marketing bhi family-friendly hoti hai jisse har age group connect kar sake, ye sab strategies milkar McDonald's ko ek reliable aur familiar brand banati hain.

Ab aate hain Red Bull par jo traditional marketing rules ko todne ke liye famous hai, Red Bull ne apni journey ek small energy drink ke roop me start ki lekin unhone kabhi apne product ko direct ads se push nahi kiya, instead unhone "content marketing" aur "event marketing" par focus kiya, Red Bull extreme sports events, stunts aur adventures ko sponsor karta hai jisse brand ka direct connection "energy" aur "fearlessness" se ban jata hai, ek example dekhiye ki jab aap Red Bull ka naam sunte hain to aapke dimaag me ek energetic aur adventurous image aati hai, ye image ads se nahi balki experiences se bani hai, Red

Bull ne apni marketing ko entertainment bana diya jisse log usse enjoy karte hain aur indirectly brand promote hota hai. Ab baat karte hain India ke powerful example Balaji Wafers ki, jiska start ek small scale business se hua tha aur aaj wo ek strong regional leader ban chuka hai, Balaji ki success ka secret hai "ground-level understanding", unhone apne target market ko deeply samjha aur uske according pricing aur distribution strategy banayi, ek real example dekhiye ki Balaji ke chips chhoti dukaanon me bhi easily available hote hain aur unka price bhi pocket-friendly hota hai jisse har class ka customer usse kharid sakta hai, Balaji ne advertising par kam aur availability par zyada focus kiya, aur isi wajah se wo quietly grow karta gaya bina flashy marketing ke, ye strategy especially small business owners ke liye ek bada lesson hai ki kabhi-kabhi simple approach hi sabse powerful hoti hai.

Ab agar hum in sab brands ki strategies ko ek saath analyse karein to kuch deep insights nikal kar aate hain jo aapke liye game-changer ho sakte hain, sabse pehla insight hai "Perception is Reality", matlab customer jo sochta hai wahi sach ban jata hai, jaise Apple premium hai kyunki log use premium samajhte hain, dusra insight hai "Consistency beats creativity",

matlab agar aap consistent nahi hain to aapka best idea bhi fail ho sakta hai, teesra insight hai "Emotion drives decision", log logic se nahi balki emotion se kharidte hain aur baad me usko justify karte hain, chautha insight hai

“Distribution is power”, agar aapka product easily available nahi hai to aapki marketing ka koi fayda nahi, aur paanchva insight hai “Brand is a long-term game”, ek strong brand ek din me nahi banta balki saalon ki mehnat aur strategy se banta hai.

Agar aap is chapter ko ek motivation ke roop me dekhein to ek bahut important baat samajh aati hai ki in sab brands ne bhi small level se start kiya tha, unke paas bhi unlimited resources nahi the lekin unhone apni strategy aur vision par focus kiya, aur aap bhi agar apne business me clarity, consistency aur customer understanding lekar aate hain to aap bhi ek strong brand build kar sakte hain, shuruaat chhoti ho sakti hai lekin soch badi honi chahiye, kyunki marketing ka asli game product bechne ka nahi balki ek aisa impression create karne ka hai jo customer ke mind me permanently reh jaaye.

Chapter: (The Ultimate Ground Marketing Blueprint)

“Brand banana ek din ka kaam nahi hota… lekin ek sahi strategy aapko pehle din se hi alag bana deti hai.”
Har successful brand ki kahani ek simple idea se start hoti hai, lekin usko reality me convert karne ke liye sirf idea nahi, **execution, consistency aur smart psychology** ki zarurat hoti hai. Bahut log business start karte hain, lekin kuch hi log brand ban pate hain, aur iska sabse bada reason hota hai — unki marketing soch.
Is chapter me hum ek aisi real-world strategy ko deep level par samjhenge jo kisi bhi beginner ko zero se uthakar ek strong brand identity tak le ja sakti hai, wo bhi bina heavy budget ke. Ye strategy sirf product bechne ki nahi, balki **logon ke dimaag me jagah banane ki strategy** hai.

Jab humne apna clothing brand start karne ka socha, tab mere mind me ek strong aur practical marketing plan already clear tha. Humne decide kiya ki hum sirf normal T-shirt ya shirt sell nahi karenge, balki apne har product ko ek premium feel ke saath present karenge, taaki jo bhi customer usse dekhe ya use kare, usse ek branded experience mile. Iske liye humne plan banaya ki har T-shirt aur shirt ko achhi tarah fold karke premium packaging me denge aur saath me ek stylish hand carry bag bhi provide karenge, jisme hamara brand name aur logo clearly print hoga, taaki jab bhi koi us bag ko lekar chale, wo automatically hamare brand ka promotion kare.

Iske baad humne apne brand ko promote karne ke liye ek unique strategy sochi, jisme humne decide kiya ki hum shuruaat me 100 T-shirts free me distribute karenge, lekin randomly nahi, balki smart targeting ke saath. Humne schools aur colleges ko target kiya, kyunki har saal waha annual exams hote hain aur har jagah kuch students aise hote hain jo 1st, 2nd aur 3rd rank laate hain. Ye students already apni achievement ki wajah se sabki nazar me hote hain, isliye humne decide kiya ki hum unhe apni taraf se free me T-shirt ya shirt denge, wo bhi complete premium packaging ke saath.

Saath hi humne ek aur powerful idea use kiya — branding banner. Jaise bade events me Bollywood stars ke peeche brand logos ka banner hota hai, waise hi hum bhi schools aur colleges me ek clean aur professional looking banner lagayenge jisme hamara brand name aur logo clearly dikhai dega. Phir hum rank holders ko us banner ke saamne khada karke unke saath photos click karenge. Isse ek simple prize distribution moment bhi ek branded photoshoot jaisa ban jayega, jisme hamara brand naturally highlight hoga.

Iske baad hum un students ko encourage karenge ki wo apni photos aur videos apne mobile se social media platforms jaise WhatsApp, Instagram aur Facebook par share karein. Hum unse kahenge ki wo ek chhota sa unboxing video bhi banayein jisme hamari T-shirt ki packaging aur brand logo clearly dikhai de. Jab ye students apni stories aur posts share karenge, to unke friends, relatives aur contacts sab isse dekhenge aur unke mind me ye impression banega ki ye koi normal product nahi, balki ek proper brand hai. Is tarah bina kisi paid advertisement ke hamara brand organically logon tak pahunchne lagega.

Is strategy ko aur strong banane ke liye humne plan kiya ki hum sirf schools aur colleges tak hi limited nahi rahenge, balki jahan jahan public gathering hoti hai, jaise mela ya fairs, waha bhi apni presence create karenge. Waha hum ek normal stall nahi, balki ek premium looking setup banayenge jo ek chhote showroom jaisa lage, jahan branding banner, proper display aur clean environment ho. Log jab is stall ko dekhenge, to unhe lagega ki ye ek serious aur professional brand hai.

Waha par hum ek engaging activity bhi introduce karenge, jaise ek simple game jiska entry fee ₹100 hoga, aur jo bhi us game ko jeetega, usse hum apni taraf se ek free branded T-shirt denge, wo bhi complete packaging ke saath. Jab koi winner banega, to us moment ko hum special banayenge — uske saath apne brand banner ke saamne photo click karenge aur usse bhi encourage karenge ki wo apni jeet aur apni T-shirt ki photo ya video social media par share kare. Isse ek excitement create hoga aur dusre log bhi attract honge.

In sab activities ko start karne se pehle hum apna online system bhi ready rakhenge, jisme ek proper website aur online store hoga jahan hamare saare products available honge. Har jagah, chahe wo school event ho ya mela stall, hum ek QR code provide karenge jise scan karke koi bhi directly hamare online store par pahunch sake. Jab log hamare brand ko dekhenge, stories me notice karenge ya live experience karenge, to wo QR code scan karke hamare products explore kar sakte hain, aur agar unhe pasand aata hai, to wo khud ke liye ya apne dosto ke liye purchase bhi karenge.

Is poore plan ka main goal simple hai — shuruaat me thoda investment karke maximum logon tak apna brand pahunchana, taaki dheere dheere log hamare brand ko pehchane, us par trust karein aur usse ek identity ke roop me accept karein. Ye strategy sirf selling ke liye nahi hai, balki ek strong brand foundation build karne ke liye hai, jahan log sirf product nahi, balki us brand ke saath judi feeling ko bhi value dete hain.

Local Event ko “Brand Event” me convert karo

Bade brands har event ko ek marketing opportunity banate hain, aur aap bhi same cheez local level par kar sakte ho. Aapko bas ek cheez karni hai — **visual presence strong banani hai**.

- Branding banner
- Logo visibility
- Organized setup
- Photo-friendly environment

☞ Example: Ek simple school prize distribution jab branding banner ke saath hota hai, to wo ek professional event jaisa lagta hai.
☞ Example: Jab students ek clean background ke saath photo lete hain jisme aapka logo clear hota hai, to wo ek mini photoshoot ban jata hai.
☞ Example: Jab ek hi jagah par multiple log aapke brand ke saath photo lete hain, to wo ek strong visual memory create karta hai.

Yaha aap ek powerful cheez build kar rahe ho — **"Visual Recall"**.

Social Media: Aapka Free ka Army

Aaj ke time me sabse bada marketing tool aapke paas already hai — *logon ka mobile phone*.
Agar aap sahi tarike se logon ko encourage karte ho, to wo khud aapka promotion karenge.
☞ Example: Ek student apni unboxing video dalta hai jisme aapka logo clearly dikh raha hota hai.
☞ Example: Ek WhatsApp status me jab koi branded bag ke saath photo dalta hai, to uske contacts us brand ko notice karte hain.
☞ Example: Ek Instagram story me tag hone se aapka brand multiple circles me reach karta hai.
☞ Example: Jab 20 log ek hi din me aapka brand post karte hain, to wo ek mini viral moment create karta hai.
Yaha aap ek system build kar rahe ho jahan **log hi aapki marketing team ban jate hain**.

Experience Marketing: "Log bhoolte nahi, feel yaad rakhte hain"

Ab aap apni strategy ko next level par le jaate ho — public engagement.
Mela, fair, ya crowded area me aap ek stall lagate ho, lekin wo normal stall nahi hota, wo ek **experience zone** hota hai.

- Clean and premium setup
- Engaging environment
- Simple game concept

☞ Example: Ek ₹100 ka game jisme winner ko branded T-shirt milti hai, logon ke liye exciting ban jata hai.
☞ Example: Jab koi jeet kar khush hota hai aur turant photo click karta hai, to wo moment emotional memory ban jata hai.
☞ Example: Jab crowd kisi ek jagah gather hota hai, to aur log automatically attract hote hain.
☞ Example: Jab log dekhte hain ki yaha kuch alag ho raha hai, to wo curiosity se khud aate hain.
Yaha aap sirf product nahi de rahe, aap **moment create kar rahe ho**.

QR Code Strategy: "Interest se Income tak ka bridge"

Marketing ka last aur sabse important step hota hai conversion.
Agar aapne attention create kar liya lekin usse sale me convert nahi kiya, to aapka effort half reh jayega.
Isliye aapko apna online system strong banana hoga.

- Website ready
- Product display clear
- Easy navigation
- QR code access

☞ Example: Ek student jo aapka banner dekh kar impress hua, wo QR scan karke directly aapke store par chala jata hai.
☞ Example: Ek mela visitor jo turant nahi kharidta, wo baad me QR ke through purchase karta hai.
☞ Example: Ek viewer jo social media par aapka brand dekhta hai, wo link ke through explore karta hai.
Yaha aap ek simple cheez kar rahe ho — **attention ko paisa me convert karna**

Investment vs Expense: Mindset ka Difference

Beginners har kharche ko loss samajhte hain, lekin smart entrepreneurs har kharche ko **investment** samajhte hain.
☞ Example: 100 free T-shirts dena ek cost nahi, ek marketing campaign hai.
☞ Example: Agar isse aapka brand 10,000 log tak pahunchta hai, to ye ek powerful exposure hai.
☞ Example: Agar unme se kuch log loyal customer ban jate hain, to aapka profit long-term me multiply hota hai.

The Ultimate Formula

Agar aap is poori strategy ko ek line me samajhna chahte ho, to yaad rakho:

“Jitna zyada log aapko dekhenge, utna zyada wo aapko yaad rakhenge… aur jitna yaad rakhenge, utna hi wo aapse kharidenge.”

Final Thought: Brand banana ek journey hai

Aapka goal sirf T-shirt bechna nahi hona chahiye, aapka goal hona chahiye:

- Log aapka naam jaane
- Log aapko pehchane
- Log aap par trust kare

☞ Example: Jab koi customer bina soche aapka brand choose karta hai, to wo aapki jeet hai.
☞ Example: Jab log dusron ko aapka brand recommend karte hain, to wo aapki growth hai.
☞ Example: Jab aapka brand ek local naam se ek identity ban jata hai, to wo aapka success hai.
“Chhote level se start karna weakness nahi hota… asli power ye hoti hai ki aap chhoti shuruaat ko kitna bada bana pate ho.”

13

Creative Marketing Ideas

Marketing ki duniya me ek baat bahut important hai — **sirf product accha hona kaafi nahi hai, logon ko uske baare me "excited" karna bhi zaroori hai**. Aaj ke time me competition itna zyada hai ki agar aap normal tarike se marketing karenge, to aap easily ignore ho sakte hain. Isi liye smart brands creative marketing ideas ka use karte hain — jisse log sirf product ko nahi dekhte, balki usko *experience* karte hain, uske baare me baat karte hain, aur dusron ko bhi batate hain.

Is chapter me hum teen powerful creative marketing strategies ko deeply samjhenge:

☞ Guerrilla Marketing

☞ Surprise Marketing

☞ Viral Marketing

Aur sabse important baat — hum inko ekdam basics se samjhenge, real-life thinking ke saath.

Creative Marketing Ideas marketing ki duniya ka wo powerful hissa hai jo ek simple product ko extraordinary bana deta hai, kyunki aaj ke highly competitive market me sirf product banana ya bechna hi kaafi nahi hota, balki us product ko is tarah present karna zaroori hota hai ki log usse notice karein, uske baare me baat karein aur usse yaad rakhein. Aaj ke time me har jagah ads hi ads hain — mobile me, road par, TV par — aur insaan ka dimaag itna overload ho chuka hai ki wo normal cheezon ko ignore kar deta hai, isi wajah se creative marketing ka importance bahut zyada badh gaya hai, kyunki ye aapko bheed se alag khada karta hai aur aapke brand ko ek unique identity deta hai.

Creative marketing ka main goal hota hai sirf bechna nahi, balki logon ko engage karna, unhe surprise karna aur unke dimaag me ek strong impression create karna, aur isi concept ke andar teen sabse important strategies aati hain — guerrilla marketing, surprise marketing aur viral marketing, jo milkar ek powerful marketing system banati hain.

Guerrilla marketing ka concept samajhne ke liye sabse pehle ye samajhna zaroori hai ki human brain unusual cheezon par turant react karta hai, yani agar aap kuch aisa karte hain jo logon ne pehle kabhi nahi dekha, to wo automatically us par dhyan denge. Guerrilla marketing ka matlab hota hai kam budget me maximum attention lena, jisme aap traditional ads ki jagah kuch aisa creative karte hain jo logon ko shock ya curiosity de.

Maan lijiye aap ek local shop chalate hain aur aap normal banner lagane ki jagah apni shop ke bahar ek aisa setup bana dete hain jo logon ko rukne par majboor kar de, jaise ek funny ya eye-catching display, to log usse dekhkar attract honge, photo lenge aur social media par share bhi karenge, aur isi tarah bina zyada paisa kharch kiye aapka promotion ho jayega. Isi strategy ka ek famous example Coca-Cola ka happiness machine campaign hai jahan unhone ek simple vending machine ko itna creative bana diya ki wo sirf cold drink dene ke bajay logon ko surprise gifts dene laga, jis se log excited ho gaye aur unhone us moment ko record karke share kar diya, aur wahi campaign viral ho gaya.

Guerrilla marketing ka sabse bada advantage ye hai ki isme creativity sabse bada investment hota hai, paisa nahi, lekin isme risk bhi hota hai kyunki agar idea clear nahi hua to log confuse ho sakte hain, isliye hamesha aisa idea choose karna chahiye jo simple ho lekin impactful ho.

Ab baat karte hain surprise marketing ki, jo ek emotional level par kaam karti hai aur customer ke saath ek strong connection banati hai. Surprise marketing ka basic funda ye hai ki customer ko wo diya jaye jo usne expect nahi kiya, kyunki jab kisi insaan ko unexpected happiness milti hai to wo us moment ko kabhi nahi bhoolta, aur wahi feeling usse brand ke saath emotionally attach kar deti hai.

Maan lijiye aap ek small food business chalate hain aur aap har 10th customer ko bina bataye ek free dessert de dete hain, to customer ke liye ye ek surprise hoga, aur wo is experience ko apne doston ke saath share karega, jisse aapka brand automatically promote ho jayega. Isi tarah Zomato aur Swiggy kabhi-kabhi apne customers ko extra items ya handwritten notes dete hain, jo chhoti si cheez hone ke bawajood ek strong emotional impact create karti hai.

Surprise marketing ka real power is baat me hai ki ye customer ko special feel karata hai, aur jab customer ko lagta hai ki usse importance di ja rahi hai, to wo brand ke saath long-term relation bana leta hai, isliye chhote-chhote gestures bhi bahut bada difference create karte hain.

Ab aate hain viral marketing par, jo aaj ke digital era ki sabse powerful strategy ban chuki hai, viral marketing ka matlab hota hai aisa content create karna jo log khud hi share karne lagein, yani aapko alag se promotion karne ki zarurat hi na pade, kyunki aapke customers hi aapke marketer ban jate hain.

Viral marketing me success tab milti hai jab aapka content emotional, funny, shocking ya relatable ho, kyunki log wahi cheezein share karte hain jo unhe feel hoti hain ya jo unhe interesting lagti hain. Maan lijiye aap apni shop ke bahar ek funny line likh dete hain jo logon ko relate ho jaye, to log uski photo lekar social media par daalenge aur wahi aapka free promotion ban jayega.

Iska ek strong example Amul hai jo har trending topic par apne creative ads banata hai aur log unhe instantly share kar dete hain, isi tarah Red Bull ne apne extreme stunts ke through apni ek unique identity banayi jo logon ke dimaag me permanently bas gayi.

Viral marketing ka sabse bada advantage ye hai ki isme aapko minimum cost me maximum reach milti hai, lekin iske liye aapko audience ki psychology samajhni padti hai aur aisa content banana padta hai jo naturally shareable ho.

Agar hum in teenon strategies ko ek saath dekhein to ye ek powerful chain ki tarah kaam karti hain jahan guerrilla marketing se attention milta hai, surprise marketing se emotional connection banta hai aur viral marketing se reach multiply ho jati hai, aur jab ye teenon ek saath use ki jati hain to ek normal business bhi ek strong brand ban sakta hai.

Creative marketing ka sabse bada rule ye hai ki log product nahi, experience kharidte hain, isliye agar aap sirf product bechne par focus karoge to aap ek normal seller banoge, lekin agar aap apne customer ko ek unique aur memorable experience doge to aap ek brand ban jaoge, aur aaj ke time me wahi brands successful hain jo logon ke dimaag ke saath-saath unke dil me bhi jagah bana lete hain.

14

Common Marketing Mistakes

Jab koi bhi insaan apna business start karta hai ya apni product/service ko market me introduce karta hai, to uska focus sirf ek cheez par hota hai — "kaise zyada se zyada logon tak pahucha jaye aur sales badhayi jaye." Lekin yahi jagah par sabse zyada galtiyaan hoti hain.

Marketing sirf promotion nahi hota, balki ek strategy, psychology aur patience ka game hota hai. Bahut log shuruaat me hi kuch aisi common mistakes kar dete hain jo unke business ko grow hone se rok deti hain. Agar aap in galtiyon ko samajh gaye, to aap dusron se bahut aage nikal sakte hain.

Sabse pehli aur sabse common galti hai **copy paste marketing**. Aaj ke time me social media par jo bhi trend chal raha hota hai, log bina soche samjhe usko copy karne lagte hain. Kisi ne Instagram par reels bana kar success pa liya, to sab wahi karne lagte hain, kisi ne ads chala kar profit kamaya, to sab wahi strategy follow karne lagte hain. Lekin yahan ek basic baat log bhool jaate hain — har business alag hota hai, har audience alag hoti hai, aur har situation bhi alag hoti hai.

Example ke liye maan lijiye ek bade brand ne funny meme marketing se apni reach badha li, to ek local shop owner bhi wahi memes use karne lagta hai, lekin uski audience us type ke content se connect hi nahi karti, result ye hota hai ki na engagement aata hai aur na hi sale hoti hai. Copy karna galat nahi hai, lekin bina samjhe copy karna sabse badi galti hai. Smart marketer wahi hota hai jo kisi strategy ko samajh kar apne business ke according modify kare.

Dusri badi galti hai **wrong audience ko target karna**. Marketing ka golden rule hai — "sabko bechne ki koshish karoge, to kisi ko bhi nahi bech paoge." Bahut log apne product ko har kisi ke liye bana dete hain, jisse unka message dilute ho jata hai. Maan lijiye aap ek premium watch sell kar rahe hain, lekin aap uska promotion un logon ke beech kar rahe hain jo budget-conscious hain, to obvious hai ki conversion nahi aayega. Isi tarah agar aap student audience ke liye product bana rahe hain aur usko corporate professionals ke saamne promote kar rahe hain, to aapka pura marketing effort waste ho jayega. Real example samajhiye — ek coaching institute ne apne ads Facebook par random audience ko target kiya, jisme har age group aur interest ke log the, result ye hua ki ad par clicks aaye lekin admission nahi hua, jab unhone specifically 16–25 age ke students ko target kiya jo competitive exams ki preparation kar rahe the, tab unka conversion dramatically increase ho gaya. Isse ek baat clear hoti hai ki sahi audience choose karna marketing ki foundation hai.

Teesri aur bahut dangerous mistake hai **patience ki kami**. Aaj ke fast world me sabko instant result chahiye, lekin marketing ek long-term game hai. Bahut log 10–15 din ads chalate hain ya social media par content dalte hain aur agar result nahi milta, to turant strategy change kar dete hain ya pura kaam hi band kar dete hain. Ye approach bilkul galat hai. Marketing me trust build hone me time lagta hai, aur bina trust ke koi bhi customer purchase nahi karta. Maan lijiye aap ek naya brand launch karte hain aur pehle hi din expect karte hain ki log aap par trust karke buy kar lenge, to ye unrealistic expectation hai. Real example dekhiye — ek small business owner ne apni product ke liye Instagram page banaya aur daily content post karne laga, pehle 2 mahine tak usko hardly koi response mila, lekin usne consistency nahi chhodi, dheere-

dheere uske followers badhne lage aur 6 mahine baad usko regular orders aane lage. Agar wo 1 mahine me hi give up kar deta, to shayad kabhi success nahi milti. Isliye patience marketing ka sabse important element hai.

Ek aur common mistake jo log aksar ignore kar dete hain wo hai **over-promotion aur under-value**. Matlab log sirf apna product bechne ki koshish karte hain, lekin customer ko value dena bhool jaate hain. Har post me "buy now", "offer khatam ho raha hai", "limited stock" likhne se log irritate ho jaate hain. Aaj ke customer smart hain, wo sirf product nahi, balki information, trust aur experience bhi chahte hain. Agar aap unhe useful content, knowledge ya entertainment provide karte hain, to wo naturally aapki taraf attract hote hain. Example ke liye agar aap fitness product sell kar rahe hain aur sirf product promote kar rahe hain, to shayad log ignore kar den, lekin agar aap daily fitness tips, diet plans aur workout videos share karte hain, to log aap par trust karenge aur eventually aapka product buy karenge.

Iske alawa ek aur mistake hoti hai **customer feedback ko ignore karna**. Bahut log apne product ya service ko perfect samajhte hain aur customer ke feedback ko importance nahi dete. Lekin reality ye hai ki market hi decide karta hai ki aapka product kitna achha hai. Agar customer kisi problem ki complaint kar raha hai aur aap usko ignore kar dete hain, to aap apne hi business ko damage kar rahe hain. Example ke liye ek restaurant owner ko baar-baar feedback mil raha tha ki uski service slow hai, lekin usne is baat ko ignore kiya, result ye hua ki dheere-dheere customers kam hote gaye, jabki agar wo us feedback par kaam karta to uska business grow kar sakta tha.

Ek subtle lekin important mistake hai **branding ko ignore karna**. Bahut log sirf product bechne par focus karte hain, lekin brand build karne par dhyan nahi dete. Branding ka matlab sirf logo ya design nahi hota, balki customer ke mind me ek image create karna hota hai. Agar aapka brand clear nahi hai, to customer aapko yaad nahi rakhega. Example ke liye agar aap ek generic product sell kar rahe hain bina kisi unique identity ke, to customer aapko kisi aur seller se differentiate nahi kar payega.

Aakhri aur sabse important baat ye samajhni hai ki marketing me galtiyaan hona normal hai, lekin unse seekhna zaroori hai. Jo log apni mistakes ko analyze karte hain aur unhe improve karte hain, wahi long-term me successful hote hain. Har failure ek feedback hota hai jo aapko better banata hai. Agar aap blindly kaam karte rahenge bina analyze kiye, to aap wahi galti baar-baar repeat karenge.

Is chapter ka essence simple hai — marketing me success sirf smart strategies se nahi, balki right mindset se aata hai. Copy karne ke bajay samajhna seekhiye, har kisi ko target karne ke bajay sahi audience par focus kariye, jaldi result ke chakkar me patience mat chhodiye, aur hamesha customer ko value dene ki koshish kariye. Agar aap in basic principles ko follow karte hain, to aap un 90% logon se alag ho jayenge jo in common mistakes ki wajah se fail ho jaate hain.

15

Building a Long-Term Brand (Final Chapter)

Jab hum business shuru karte hain, tab aksar hamara focus sirf ek cheez par hota hai — "kaise jaldi se sales badhayein?" Lekin sach ye hai ki jo business sirf short-term profit ke peeche bhaagte hain, wo zyada time tak tik nahi paate. Ek strong aur successful business banane ke liye sabse important cheez hoti hai — **long-term brand banana**. Brand sirf ek naam ya logo nahi hota, balki wo trust, feeling aur experience hota hai jo log aapke business ke saath jodte hain.

Is final chapter me hum samjhenge ki kaise aap ek aisa brand bana sakte hain jo sirf aaj nahi, balki saalon tak logon ke dimaag aur dil me rahe.

Trust Build Karna — Brand ki Sabse Strong Foundation

Trust bina koi bhi brand zyada door tak nahi ja sakta. Aap chahe kitni bhi marketing kar lo, agar customer ko aap par bharosa nahi hai, to wo ek baar purchase karega aur phir kabhi wapas nahi aayega. Trust build karna ek din ka kaam nahi hota, ye ek process hai jo dheere dheere develop hota hai.

Sabse pehla step hota hai **honesty**. Aap jo bolte ho, wo deliver karo. Agar aap product ke bare me kuch promise kar rahe ho, to wo exactly waisa hi hona chahiye. Jaise ek local shopkeeper agar customer ko bolta hai ki "ye shirt pure cotton hai" aur wo actually synthetic nikalti hai, to customer turant samajh jata hai aur phir kabhi wapas nahi aata, lekin agar wo sach bolta hai ki "ye mix fabric hai lekin durable hai aur sasta bhi hai" to customer ko trust feel hota hai.

Dusra important factor hai **consistency**. Agar aap kabhi achha product dete ho aur kabhi average, to trust break ho jata hai. Customer ko ye feel hona chahiye ki har baar jab wo aapke paas aayega, usse same quality milegi. Jaise agar koi chai wala har din same taste ki chai deta hai, to log us par depend karne lagte hain.

Teesra factor hai **customer support**. Agar product me problem aati hai aur aap usko solve karte ho, to trust aur strong ho jata hai. Example ke liye agar kisi ne online product kharida aur wo defective nikla, lekin seller ne bina sawal ke replace kar diya, to customer future me bhi usi seller se kharidega.

Trust build karne ka ek hidden rule hai — **"pehle do, phir lo"**. Matlab aap pehle value do, help karo, knowledge share karo, phir sale apne aap aayegi. Jaise koi person Instagram par free tips deta hai business ke bare me aur logon ki help karta hai, dheere dheere log us par trust karne lagte hain aur jab wo paid course launch karta hai, to log bina hesitation ke buy karte hain.

Brand Reputation — Aapki Image Jo Logon Ke Dimaag Me Hai

Brand reputation wo hoti hai jo log aapke bare me dusron ko batate hain. Aap khud apne brand ke bare me kuch bhi bol sakte ho, lekin asli reputation tab banti hai jab log aapke liye bolte hain.

Reputation build karne ke liye sabse important cheez hai **customer experience**. Agar aapka customer experience achha hai, to log automatically aapki tarif karenge. Jaise agar koi restaurant customer ko sirf khana nahi, balki ek achha environment aur respect deta hai, to customer apne friends ko bhi recommend karta hai.

Aaj ke time me reputation ka ek bada part hai **online presence**. Reviews, ratings, comments — ye sab milkar aapki image banate hain. Agar aapke paas positive reviews hain, to naye customers ko confidence milta hai. Lekin agar negative reviews hain aur aap unhe ignore karte ho, to wo aapki brand image ko damage karte hain.

Yahan ek smart strategy hoti hai — **negative feedback ko opportunity samajhna**. Agar koi customer complain karta hai, to use ignore mat karo, balki solve karo aur publicly show karo ki aapne problem fix ki. Jaise agar kisi ne comment kiya ki "delivery late thi" aur aap reply karte ho ki "sorry for inconvenience, next time hum fast delivery ensure karenge" aur phir aap waise hi karte ho, to dusre logon ko lagta hai ki ye brand responsible hai.
Reputation ka ek aur important aspect hai **values**. Aapka brand kis cheez ke liye khada hai? Kya aap quality ke liye known ho? Ya affordability ke liye? Ya innovation ke liye? Jab aap apni values clear rakhte ho aur un par stick karte ho, to log aapko usi identity ke saath yaad rakhte hain.

Jaise ek small business agar decide karta hai ki wo "best quality at fair price" dega, aur wo consistently wahi karta hai, to dheere dheere uski reputation strong ho jati hai ki "yahan se liya hua product reliable hota hai".

Long-Term Thinking — Real Game Yahin Se Start Hota Hai

Short-term thinking me log quick profit dekhte hain, lekin long-term thinking me log **relationship aur sustainability** dekhte hain. Agar aap har decision ye soch kar lete ho ki "iska 5 saal baad kya effect hoga?", to aap automatically ek strong brand bana rahe ho.

Long-term thinking ka matlab hota hai ki aap **customer lifetime value** ko samjho. Ek customer sirf ek baar ka sale nahi hota, wo multiple baar aapke paas aa sakta hai. Isliye ek baar zyada profit kamane ke chakkar me customer ko cheat karna ek bada loss hai.

Jaise agar koi shopkeeper ek product me ₹200 extra kama leta hai galat information dekar, to shayad usko ek baar profit mil jaye, lekin wo customer hamesha ke liye chala jata hai, jabki agar wo honestly ₹50 kam profit le aur customer ko satisfy kare, to wo customer baar baar aayega aur total profit zyada hoga.

Long-term thinking me ek aur important cheez hai **brand building over selling**. Har baar direct sell mat karo. Kabhi kabhi sirf connect karo, educate karo, entertain karo. Jaise social media par agar aap sirf "buy now, buy now" karoge to log ignore karenge, lekin agar aap useful content share karoge, to log aapko follow karenge aur jab aap sell karoge, to wo interested honge.

Iska ek simple example hai — ek clothing seller agar sirf products post karta hai, to engagement kam hoti hai, lekin agar wo styling tips, fashion ideas aur customer stories share karta hai, to log uske saath connect karte hain aur brand strong hota ha

Emotional Connection — Brand Ko Dil Se Jodna

Long-term brand sirf product se nahi banta, wo **emotion se banta hai**. Jab customer aapke brand ke saath emotionally connect ho jata hai, to wo price ya alternatives nahi dekhta. Jaise koi customer ek specific shop se isliye kharidta hai kyunki us shopkeeper ka behavior achha hai aur wo respect deta hai, even agar dusri jagah same product sasta mile, tab bhi wo wahi se kharidega.
Emotion create karne ke liye aapko **storytelling** use karna chahiye. Apne brand ki story batayein — aapne kaise start kiya, kya struggle tha, aapka mission kya hai. Log stories se connect karte hain, products se nahi.

Patience — Sabse Underrated Skill

Long-term brand banana ek marathon hai, sprint nahi. Isme time lagta hai, consistency lagti hai aur patience sabse important hota hai.
Aksar log 3–6 mahine me result na milne par give up kar dete hain. Lekin jo log patience rakhte hain aur continuously improve karte hain, wahi successful hote hain. Jaise ek YouTube creator shuru me videos daalta hai aur views nahi aate, lekin wo consistently quality content daalta rehta hai, dheere dheere uska audience build hota hai aur phir ek time aata hai jab uska channel grow karta hai.

Final Insight — Brand Ek Investment Hai

Agar simple words me samjhein, to brand building ek **long-term investment** hai. Aaj jo efforts aap daalte ho — achha product, achha service, honest communication — uska result aapko future me milta hai.
Ek strong brand ka sabse bada fayda ye hota hai ki aapko har baar new customers ke liye struggle nahi karna padta, balki customers khud aapke paas aate hain aur dusron ko bhi laate hain.

Chapter Conclusion

Is pure journey ka essence ye hai ki business me sirf paisa kamana goal nahi hona chahiye, balki **value create karna, trust build karna aur relationship banana** hona chahiye. Jab aap ye mindset adopt karte ho, to aapka brand naturally grow karta hai.
Yaad rakhiye —
Product log ek baar kharidte hain, lekin brand ko baar baar choose karte hain.
Agar aapne trust build kar liya, strong reputation bana li aur long-term thinking adopt kar li, to aapka brand sirf ek business nahi rahega, balki ek identity ban jayega — jo time ke saath aur strong hoti jayegi.
Yahi ek successful aur sustainable business ki asli pehchaan hai.

Timeless Wisdom for Success

Sapne wo nahi jo aap sote waqt dekhte ho, sapne wo hote hain jo aapko sone nahi dete.
— A. P. J. Abdul Kalam
Agar aap bada soch sakte ho, to aap bada kar bhi sakte ho.
— Donald Trump
Success unhi ko milti hai jo risk lene ki himmat rakhte hain.
— Elon Musk
Har chhoti shuruaat ek bade result ka foundation hoti hai.
— Jeff Bezos
Aapka attitude hi aapki direction decide karta hai.
— Warren Buffett
Jo log mehnat se dosti kar lete hain, wo kabhi fail nahi hote.
— Ratan Tata
Sapne tab tak sach nahi hote jab tak aap action nahi lete.
— Tony Robbins
Aap jitna seekhte ho, utna hi aap grow karte ho.
— Bill Gates
Fear se aage hi real growth hoti hai.
—
Consistency hi success ka sabse bada secret hai.
— Dhirubhai Ambani
Aapka future aapke aaj ke decisions par depend karta hai.
— Brian Tracy

Kabhi bhi apne goals chhote mat rakho, warna result bhi chhota milega.
— Arnold Schwarzenegger
Har problem ek hidden opportunity lekar aati hai.
— Steve Jobs
Agar aap khud par believe karte ho, to duniya bhi karegi.
— Oprah Winfrey
Time waste karna sabse bada loss hota hai.
— Benjamin Franklin
Discipline bina success sirf ek sapna hai.
— Jocko Willink
Aapka network hi aapki net worth hota hai.
— Porter Gale
Har din thoda better banne ki koshish karo.

—

Jo log give up nahi karte, wahi history banate hain.
— Narendra Modi
Ideas sabke paas hote hain, execution hi farq laata hai.
— Mark Zuckerberg
Success ek journey hai, destination nahi.
— Zig Ziglar
Aapka comfort zone hi aapki growth ka sabse bada enemy hai.
— Robin Sharma
Jo aaj mushkil lag raha hai, kal aapki strength banega.
— Robert Kiyosaki

Focus karo, distraction khud hi kam ho jayega.
— Cal Newport
Bada banne ke liye bada sochna zaroori hai.
— Andrew Carnegie
Har din ek naya chance hai apne aapko improve karne ka.
— Mel Robbins
Failure sirf ek lesson hai, end nahi.
— Henry Ford
Aapki habits hi aapka future banati hain.
— Stephen Covey
Jo log wait karte hain, unhe sirf utna milta hai jitna try karne wale chhod dete hain.
— Abraham Lincoln

Thank You

Aapka dil se shukriya…
Is kitab ko yahan tak padhne ke liye sirf time hi nahi, balki aapne apna focus, patience aur learning mindset bhi invest kiya hai — aur ye hi wo quality hai jo kisi bhi insaan ko life me aage le jaati hai.
Ye book sirf marketing ya business ke concepts samjhane ke liye nahi likhi gayi thi, balki ek aisi soch develop karne ke liye likhi gayi hai jisse aap apni life me kuch bada kar sakein. Agar aapne is kitab se ek bhi idea seriously samjha aur use real life me apply kiya, to samajh lijiye iska purpose successful ho gaya.
Yeh safar yahin khatam nahi hota…
Asli journey ab start hoti hai.
Ab aapke paas knowledge hai — lekin success tab milega jab aap action loge. Chhote chhote steps uthaiye, galtiyan kariye, seekhiye aur improve kariye. Yaad rakhiye, har bada brand aur har successful insaan ek chhoti shuruaat se hi start hua tha.
Agar kabhi aapko lage ki progress slow hai ya result nahi aa raha, to give up mat kariyega. Consistency aur patience hi wo secret hai jo aapko dusron se alag banata hai.
Main dil se dua karta hoon ki aap apne goals achieve karein, apna ek strong brand banayein aur apni ek alag pehchaan create karein.
Aap sirf ek reader nahi ho…
Aap ek future creator ho.

Phir milenge kisi naye idea, naye concept aur naye safar ke saath…
Once again, Thank You So Much!

www.ingramcontent.com/pod-product-compliance
Lightning Source LLC
LaVergne TN
LVHW090533110826
845146LV00003B/1083

* 9 7 8 9 3 5 8 9 0 5 8 7 8 *